Rajput

Eva Ulian

WestBow
PRESS

WestBow Press books may be ordered through booksellers or by contacting:

WestBow Press
A Division of Thomas Nelson
1663 Liberty Drive
Bloomington, IN 47403
www.westbowpress.com
1-(866) 928-1240

Because of the dynamic nature of the Internet, any Web addresses or links contained in this book may have changed since publication and may no longer be valid. The views expressed in this work are solely those of the author and do not necessarily reflect the views of the publisher, and the publisher hereby disclaims any responsibility for them.

ISBN: 978-1-4497-0060-7 (sc)
ISBN: 978-1-4497-0061-4 (e)

Library of Congress Control Number: 2010924399

Printed in the United States of America

WestBow Press rev. date: 3/4/2010

TABLE OF CONTENTS

PART ONE

Part one of the history is based on historical records available in Rajasthan from which the Studio of the Architect Remo Serafin, Italy, commissioned to restore Gogunda Palace compiled its historical research.

Preface

Much of Mewar's history has survived in the written form due to being the seat of the highest ranking Ruler in India, namely, the Maharana. This is not the case for lesser territories, districts, and Rajput communities in Rajasthan or throughout India, where little if any written history is available.

Therefore fate would have it that thanks to Mewar's interaction with other Regions it was possible to trace events that touched various Rajput communities: the Paramara Rajputs in Malwa, now known as the Pradesh area, South East of Mewar; the Rathore Rajputs in Marwar, now Jodhpur in the North West; the Chauhan Rajputs in Delhi, in the North being the first to be overcome by the Muslim Empire; and finally the Solanki Rajputs in Gujarat, in the South West, from whence the Sisodian Rajputs of Mewar and consequently the Jhala Rajputs of Gogunda originate.

Thus, when the **Architect Remo Serafin** of A.R.S. Studio in Treviso, Italy was given the task to restore the Royal Raja Palace of Gogunda, whose restoration drawing was chosen as the front piece of this work, it was to be expected, that the historical research to be compiled for the restoration purposes would have to be made from scratch.

The only written records available were a list of Rajas who occupied the throne of Gogunda, even so, there were no dates as to their relevant births or deaths let alone when they actually reigned. It therefore soon became apparent that it was not customary for historical events to be committed to the written word, but throughout the ages, such transmission occurred, by word of mouth.

This was so, except for one fortunate occasion, the unearthing of "The Khyat." Having discovered that the villagers of Gogunda possessed a written record, even if somewhat limited, of events that occurred in the area during the last two centuries was something quite remarkable indeed.

The Khyat came into existence thanks to a request made by Maharana Sajjan Singh of Mewar (1874-1884) that the people of Gogunda should write down their history which was compiled in the Mewari language by an Audhichya Brahmin in the form of a poem and structures the basis for the second part of this history. The first part of the history is based on historical records available in Rajasthan from which the Studio of Architecture commissioned to restore Gogunda Palace compiled its historical research.

The author therefore wishes to thank the **Architect Remo Serafin** of the said Studio for allowing access and use of such research.

The Appendixes at the back of this work are the lists of simultaneous Rulers who reigned in the areas being dealt with in the history, which again is an innovation, resulting from the above mentioned research.

Eva Ulian
1st January 2010
http://www.eva-ulian.eu/

PART ONE

Part one of the history is based on historical records available in Rajasthan from which the Studio of the Architect Remo Serafin, Italy, commissioned to restore Gogunda Palace compiled its historical research.

CHAPTER ONE

Prophecy of Harit Rishi[1]

The Hand That Holds The Sword Shall Rule A Kingdom

The 7th Guhilot Ruler is murdered: Prince Kalbhoj taken to safety

NAGDA 716 AD

Silent they were. Their footsteps glided through the stone corridors weightless. Darkened figures with eyes gleaming in the night moved stealthily but not hurriedly; they were no strangers, they knew Nagda[2] Palace well… they felt safe. They slithered through to the Rawal's[3] quarters and crept behind the tiger skin clad sentinels planting a dagger in the swarthy flesh before the Bhils[4] could utter a single cry. But for the Rawal they saved the best cut, slashing his throat and severing his head from his torso, snatching it by the hair and holding it up above the bed. Seemingly there were no witnesses, no eyes to tell who had done the deed. The small bodies of the Bhils lay buried in their blood. Behind the shroud of the Rawal's bed a Bhil, not yet a man, had been woken by a movement in the drape, he slithered on his stomach past the opening at the side and ran to his Mistress' quarters. The Guhilot[5] Prince, Kalbhoj, had to be saved.

The faithful Bhil had reached his Queen's apartment and lifted the stone from the floor. The Queen snatched the young child from his bed

---

1   Was the sage who prophesied Kalbhoj would rule Mewar after been given the sword by the hermit Gorakhnath, that severed rocks c 725 AD
2   The capital of Mewar at the time
3   Ruler- at the time Mahendra II 688-716- former title of Raja
4   Mountain inhabitants, protectors of the Rawal whom they anoint with the blood from their thumb
5   Forerunner of the Sisodia Dynasty

and placed it in the Bhil's arms who with the speed of a hare disappeared beneath the hole. The Queen dragged the stone back in its place, took one of the torches of fire and set it next to the drapes, then lying on her bed waited for the flames to consume her.

Eighteen Years Later- Chittor
Prince Kalbhoj Guhilot regains Chittorgarh: founds the Mewar Dynasty as Bappa Rawal

A group of horses with the dusky, small figures of the Bhils upon their backs raced through the plains into the raven night leaving the imperious Aravalli[6] hills behind them. One of the horsemen, however, stood shoulders above the rest and his skin, even in the darkness glimmered a lighter shade. The horsemen had bows and arrows on their backs but he, a sword by his side; flashing in the folds of the dark, striking lightning as he fled. The dawn grew light and the shadows of the dark were no more as they reached the City[7], the tall man upon the silver steed, had come to take.

The crowds were out in their full force that day. The Ruler from the neighbouring realm, Malwa,[8] Maun Mori, had come to celebrate the expansion of his kingdom which had eaten away much of the land called Mewar pertaining to the once Guhilot[9] Ruler. But as there no longer existed a Guhilot Ruler since the Usurper years before had severed the head of the last Guhilot, no one had really occupied the throne officially, much to the pleasure of Maun Mori in spite that his sister, the Guhilot Queen had set fire to herself to save the Crown Prince, which Maun Mori was sure had not survived, therefore, leaving no obstacles on the road to the conquest of Nagda, the once Guhilot capital. Hence occupying the city of Chittor in Mewar, the land of the Guhilot, was for Maun Mori an immense feat since he had been able to construct the most magnificent fort, namely Chittorgarh,[10] of which in the whole of India, there was no comparison.

Much bustle and ado was concentrated on the plain below the fortress of Chittor around an iron pillar containing inscriptions that no one could decipher. The Bhils tied their horses and mingled in the festive crowd

6   Chain of mountains which runs for 600 km across the State of Rajasthan where the native Bhils often protected the Mewar Ruler
7   Chittor- 150 km NW of Nagda- Northern end of Aravallis
8   Now, Madhya Pradesh
9   From GUHIL the First Ruler of Mewar- 569-603
10   Garth = Fort

when an even greater flutter arose, again in the direction of the pole. A procession of horsemen strode forth in majestic gallop led by an elephant covered handsomely with gold and purple velvet bearing a figure that did not stir. Presently beside the pole the procession halted and from his lofty position Maun Mori began to speak:

"To any man who can cut our ancient fathers' pillar with a sword, I will give half of the Kingdom of Mewar." The crowds bustled around but no one spoke which was what Maun Mori had expected- however, if no one came forth with a claim it was not an unmistakable sign that the people of Mewar had fully, and without question accepted the Malwa Ruler as their conqueror. Again Maun Mori spoke; "Half the Kingdom of Mewar…"

"You cannot give to others what is not yours, Sire." the tall man surrounded by the Bhils called out in a more resounding voice than the Ruler of Malwa had done. The people turned to one another in astonishment, the Ruler looked down consternated. The first set of guards moved towards the man, the Bhils swished out their arrows in a flash, the Ruler signalled the guards to retreat.

"Let's see what the stranger has to say for himself before putting him in chains." The Ruler of Malwa informed the guards.

"I am no stranger Sire, I am your nephew…"

"Nephew? I have no nephew that bears my name?"

"Not yours Sire, but that of your sister's husband."

"The Guhilot!"

"I am Crown Prince Kalbhoj Guhilot! And now Lord of Mewar, the Mewar that had been usurped from me and which you have since possessed." The crowd nodded in support of the stranger also because they never had the desire to have a Ruler from another Kingdom lording it over them: having an authentic Ruler from Mewar itself was more than the people could hope for. Maun Mori sensed the surge of affection that the young prince had evoked in the people.

"My dear nephew, I cannot be held at fault for giving a leader to a leaderless kingdom." He paused to see if his words were gaining favour, "Bear in mind Nephew, that those who slaughtered your father, deprived my noble Rajput family of a sister too." This the uncle had shrewdly said so as not to have suspicion fall upon him.

"It did not occur to myself," Kalbhoj smiled with irony, "that you would ever have commissioned that little affair some years back, Uncle. Nevertheless my Mother, or if you think best, your sister, did marry into a family no less noble or no less Rajput…" Kalbhoj paused and looked up

5

wryly, "however, the lands of Mewar made the sorrow of losing a sister less painful, I don't doubt." Maun Mori smiled nervously. "Half the Kingdom of Mewar, did you say, Uncle?" Kalbhoj laughed with scorn, "I'm in the mood to be generous, Uncle." He climbed a boulder next to the pillar and faced the crowd, "My uncle and I will give half of MY Kingdom to whoever can splice this pillar…" he looked around, "who will be first?" The crowd stood still in silence. "Is there not one who wants half a kingdom?" Again no one moved. "In that case I will do it myself," Kalbhoj pulled out the gleaming sword from beneath his belt and held it vertically between his forehead.

"Wait!" his uncle cried, "is it not best to test the sword first nephew?" Kalbhoj laughed.

"Why Uncle, do you suspect it has been Jinxed?"

"Indeed not, Nephew, but rumour has it that the gods have invested a cow-herd with a sword – a special sword!"

"Really Uncle, surely you don't believe in magic?" Again the uncle smiled nervously.

"No, indeed. But it costs nothing to be prudent, does it now?"

" Very well Uncle,"

Kalbhoj placed the sword length wise along his arm, the weighty handle facing the crowd. Maun Mori gave a serious nod towards the far end of the crowd and a semi-giant made his way through the masses who stepped back to make way for the lengthy strides as he stepped forward. The semi-giant bowed before the Ruler and then taking the sword held it up high and with the mighty strength that threatened to burst his veins he let it fall with a blow that clanged throughout the plain. Again he tried, this time the blow produced a zigzagging blister of fire that it seemed lighting had struck. The semi-giant tried again and again until he fell smouldering in a pool of sweat. "Are you satisfied, Uncle, that the sword is perfectly safe, not tampered by the demons or the gods?" The crowds shouted an uproar of approval and the guards began to relax their stand.

"You have charmed my people, not the sword," the Uncle said even against his better judgement, allowing himself to be taken in by the impudence of the Lad.

"So, now, you will allow me to try, will you not Uncle?" He could not refuse. Kalbhoj took the sword, placed it high above his head and struck, the crowd gasped- nothing happened. The Bhils however were not gasping, they were not at all concerned, busily sharpening their arrows they were. Kalbhoj took up the sword again and placed it upright between his eyes, then swiftly struck the pillar which immediately fell, spliced in two by the sword. Not a sound, not a limb stirred, the astonished Ruler sat as if castrated on mountainous elephant. Suddenly a joyous cry broke throughout the plain. The guards took Kalbhoj and carried him shoulder high, and as they passed the side of the elephant, the Uncle leaned downwards and muttered: "It was magic, after all!"

"There is no magic in my sword, Uncle," Kalbhoj winked cheekily. "Say rather, the iron was not as solid as you thought!" And with that, in the year of Our Lord seven hundred and thirty four, Kalbhoj, the cowherd that was, but a successor of the First Ruler, Guhil, became the VIII Guhilot Ruler and the Founder of the Mewar Dynasty, to be known by future generations as Bappa Rawal.

CHAPTER TWO

Bappa Rawal's Ancestors and Successors

Gujarat, their land of origin: the fate of Bappa Rawal's uncle Mori and his kingdom, Malwa (now Pradesh);17th Ruler of Mewar loses Chittor to Malwa; the Ghazanvid Empire takes root in Sindh; origins of the Makwana Rajputs

Having dutifully deposed his Uncle, Bappa Rawal left Nagda and transferred the royal quarters to Chittor which he made the capital of Mewar. Indeed, even though much against his will, as Bappa Rawal's dream had been to return to the land of his ancestor the first Ruler, Guhil, who had ruled in Idar outside the south west border of Mewar in what is called Gujarat. There, Guhil had formed the headquarters of his kingdom in his native land and from noble Rajput stock two centuries previously.

The III Ruler suffered the same fate as Bappa Rawal's father, murdered by unknown hands forcing the IV Ruler to abandon Idar and seek another capital elsewhere which was Nagda. However, it was impossible for Bappa Rawal to even contemplate the thought of regaining Idar: Gujarat, was under siege by the invaders from Kabul sweeping out all those of Rajput descent. Neither was Bappa Rawal for a moment immune from these invaders but whether it was because he had already been rubbed up the wrong way by what they did to his ancestor or because the Rajputs that had been ousted from their own kingdoms found refuge in Rajputana[11] and gave their full strength to the Ruler; Bappa Rawal fared much better than his neighbours in Gujarat and was able to push back the invaders beyond the western borders of Mewar- thus, practically sending them back where they came from.

---

11   The name which referred to the area Bappa Rawal founded as Mewar and conse-quently became known as Rajasthan

Of course Bappa Rawal also fared much better than his Uncle Mori's Kingdom of Malwa. Having been deposed by his nephew did little for Maun Mori's credibility leaving the door open to be swept out by the Pratihara Dynasty from Kannauj near Agra- in spite of the fact that they too were Rajputs but having a ruler on the throne of Malwa that could easily be out done by a cowherd, was too much of what seemed to the Pratihars's as a good opportunity to pass by.

Indeed, the Pratihas were an Empire of sorts which lasted three hundred years, but not in Malwa where they survived barely fifty years before being overcome by yet another cast of Rajputs, the Paramaras. But the Paramara Rajputs meant business and the inborn belief that a Rajput was the son of a king, as the name implies, with the ultimate right to conquer what ever lands are available but for the taking, was soon put into practice. Thus the VI Ruler of Malwa Siyaka II takes Chittor forcing the 17th Ruler of Mewar Allat Singh to find another abode, which he did do a hundred kilometres south west at Ahar, next to the old capital of Nagda. It seems however that no great enmity was caused between the two rulers because even though Allat came to the throne of Mewar in 951 and ruled only for two years before the Malwa ruler took over, it cannot be taken for granted that he was killed- it was not easy to dispense of a strong hefty man like Allat who sent to the ageless kingdom up above Devpala a Pratihara ruler who having had his kingdom taken by the Paramaras thought well to see what he could grab in Mewar, but alas for him he did not count on having to come to terms with the 'giant' Allat.

Allat may have been throne less but there is the possibility that he remained much alive and working alongside the Paramara Ruler to fight off the many threats of invaders taking over the land, that is, the whole of the land or at any rate, anything that was exposed to the taking. There is even an inscription that states that the Paramara Bhoja I of Malwa was aided and abetted by a Guhil Prince and although this takes place sixty years later, it would not be a surprise that Allat started such a tradition. Even though there was a Paramara Ruler on the throne of Chittor this did not mean that Mewar had ceased to exist, the Rulers continued to come forward fast and foremost on the throne of Ahar and without any disdain in pooling together all the Rajput forces in order to overcome Mahmud of Ghazni from Afghanistan who two years earlier in 1005 had already conquered Sindh, just on the western border of Mewar; the invaders were certainly getting close.

The gathering together of all Rajput forces with their thirty one different clans in this particular case is the exception that confirms the rule. The sad state of affairs to find that the only thing in common that Rajputs had, seemed to have been the antagonism for one another however, may find some consolation that it was not only Rajputs who fought other Rajputs or that Rajputs fought the invaders, but the foreign invaders themselves had to fight off Rajput forces who invaded their lands. This was so in a place called Sindh in Pakistan where the Ghaznavid Empire took roots. Sometime on the threshold of the first millennium, in the vicinity of the Kithar Range Mountains in Sindh, the Makwana clan of Rajputs made their above under the first known Ruler Vehisadeva succeeded by his son Kersadeva. And when their neighbours the Afghanistans placed one of their Rulers in Sindh, the Makwanas were not at all in agreement. Consequently, somewhere in the year1090, the then Makwana Ruler Kersadeva gathered together his best steed and decided to pay a visit himself to the then Sindh Ruler who must have been Duda I if it was before 1092 or Singhar if it was later.

The sultry ground was lost in darkness. The Makwana warriors slithered on their horses without a sound. A streak of blood outlined the sky. They had to move before the people woke. They had to strike while the silence of the earth buried all in sleep. They would make that sleep eternal. None would wake where Makwana's chief, Kesardeva passed. He would strike off Sindh's head and place it on a stake. He would take the land and make it his own dwelling place. Sindh would be theirs. That the Makwana warriors would do. They would no longer need to grovel like vagabonds in the sullen Kithar Range, this Kesardeva swore. Kesardeva, son of the first Makwana Chief, the great Vehiasdeva, would leave the conquered land to his son Harpaldeva, and to his sons after him. He would gain this land, at whatever cost, even that of his very life.

The sound of hoofs was like whispers blowing through the parched ground. Under the ink darkness of a breathless sky, all was motionless except for the whistling sound of the hoofs sweeping towards the village. The first row of warriors lit their torches; the rest unsheathed their glimmering sword. As the torches fell unto the tents, huts and shacks a sudden flame burst into the sky. Shrill cries of "The Makwanas! The Makwanas!" pierced the air. The Sindh fighters sprung from their sleep bared their breasts as the Makwanas thrust their swords in them. Kesardeva flashed his eyes into the blaze lit night, the Ruler- the Sindh Ruler was not in sight. Bodies were scattered at his feet as the encampment burned, his horse neighed wildly and leap up, Kesardeva pulled the reins and with a wry smile of defeat turned the horse around- The Sindh ruler had slipped away, fled to the safety of the hills. "To Mewar and the Guhilot!" Kesardeva ordered his son Harpaldeva, the unsheathed sword pointing towards Thar, The Great Indian Desert ahead.

Kesardeva sat upright and unflinching on his horse. Harpaldeva looked at his father, "You are not coming?"

"And let that beast live to hound me again!"

"I will not go. I will stay and fight with you." But Harpaldeva's father shook his head,

"I forbid it. We are sons of kings, Rajputs. And the place of a Rajput is at the service of his Rawal. Mewar is ravaged by the Muslims. It has already lost its great capital Chittor.

"We will regain it..."

"And what is left- plundered by Marathas- they are the worst to fight... our own kind, Hindu warriors like ourselves."

"No, father, not like ourselves. We do not plunder; we fight honourably, show mercy to the enemy- we are Rajputs" Harpalveda turned his horse to face his father. "Send my brothers to the Solanki court in Gujarat, at least the Solanki Royal house have manage to free themselves from the fetters of Kabul. I will stay beside you."

But fate reversed itself on that mortal dawn- it was the ruler of Sindh who crept inside Kesardeva's tent and thrust a dagger into the Mawkwana's breast. Woken by the noise, Harpalveda rushed to his father's side.

"Flee, my son, flee to south across the Great Desert, flee to Gujarat," the dying Kesardeva breathed. "There the land is moist and green- there Harpalveda will give sons who will be great warriors, great Rajputs and you will father a line of Kings..." With his father's unfinished words thundering in his heart, Harpalveda plunged into the fiery dawn of the Great Desert.

CHAPTER THREE

Strife only Strife

Harpalveda flees to the Solanki Rajput leader in Gujarat and gains Chittor from Malwa: founds the Jhala Rajput clan and the state of Jhalawad: a family split occurs in the Guhilot Dynasty; the massacre of Chauhan[12] Rajput Ruler of Delhi Prithviraj III by Mohammed from Ghur; an attempt to wipe out Rajput existence

Once in Gujarat, Harpalveda took refuge at the court of Karnadeva Solanki Rajput whose dynasty had been founded by Mulraj almost a century back, after much ado in getting rid of invaders from Kabul. The aging Karnadeva was not too pleased to hear that his family's greatest foe, had also taken Kiranti, exterminating Harpaldeva's entire clan of Rajputs; not so much because he was particularly fond of Harpaldeva and his family but because without them to shield Gujarat from Sindh there remained only the empty Thar Desert which in effect made the invaders only some horse gallops away. The only outcome that could possibly come of this was to shower Harpaldeva with a number of villages and expect some return in battle when the opportune time came.

The time indeed came when after the death of Karnadeva, his son Jayasinh took the throne of Gujarat in 1094. Harpaldeva had hardly the time to settle down in his new abode when the young Gujarat Ruler set him head of an army to fight the foe which in this case was not Kabul, but Rajputs like themselves from Malwa- the prize at stake, Chittor. Harpaldeva was not much updated on the events of which ruler or not sat on the throne of Chittor, he was there to serve his Protector with the hope

---

12 One of the four Rajput dynasties (the other three are: Pratiharas, Paramaras and Solankis)

that he would have his own kingdom himself one day, should he do well enough to take lands in abundance for his Lord.

Harpaldeva served majestically: regaining Chittor, the great Mewar Capital that had been lost to the Raj of Malwa in 1051. In recognition for this gallant action, Jaysinh Solanki showered 1,800 villages in Jalawar and 500 villages in Bhal to Harpalveda. So now this brave Rajput was indeed a Lord and took a Solanki wife, given to him by the Solanki Ruler. Thus he possessed a royal residence at Patdi and a royal wife; he had a kingdom, he was a Lord and a Ruler, but as yet had no name; he did not possess a clan, his had been exterminated back in Sindh.

One day Harpalveda's children were playing in the courtyard when an elephant broke in and was about to trample the children to death when his Solanki Rani,[13] snatched them quickly away. This was interpreted as the gods looking benevolently on Makwana descendants and were given the name Jhala, meaning 'snatched up'. Hence the Jhalawad state was born.

Somewhere around the third decade of the 12th century, Harpalveda dies and is succeeded by Sodho Ji, the first of his twelve sons, but for his kingdom and the many more that were to follow, nothing is known about the descendants of Harpalveda except that since Gujarat fell into Muslim hands, the Jhala dynasty too would have had to succumb to the foreign dominion- which as can be imagined, the Jhala warriors did not take too kindly to.

All this pulling and tugging over Chittor between Gujarat and Malwa, Gujarat fortified with the newborn Jhalawad state, was not strongly opposed by Mewar, in effect it was well tolerated, because Mewar, having problems of their own, thought it best to place others in charge of that magnificent invincible fort Chittorgarh; warriors who were flesh of their own flesh, Rajputs and Hindu; instead of letting it fall into foreign hands and of Muslim creed. When the founder of the Kingdom of Mewar, Bappa Rawal was wandering in the forests of the Aravallis his master, the sage Harit Rishi taught his disciple that who ever would sit on the throne that the sword would bring to rule would be the caretaker of that Kingdom for the supreme Lord of Mewar is the Hindu god Ekling Ji[14] himself.

Bappa Rawal and all the Rulers after him, although crowned with the insignia of royalty, have never taken the place of their Deity but acted as Trustees for the Lord of Mewar, Eckling Ji. And of course, Malwa and

---

13   Rajput Queen
14   A manifestation of the Hindu god Shiva, more precisely, the life-giving phallic symbol of Shiva

Gujarat thought the same, best keep the fortress in secure Rajput hands than to let it fall into hands unknown, even though this hardly explains why the two Rajput clans, Malwa and Gujarat, decided to go to war over its possession. However this had little consequence on Mewar which paid modest attention to the matter since they had to cope with much more important problems from within- namely a family split.

The father was Karan I who reigned between 1158-1168 with certainty; what is not so certain is what happened to his two older sons since, at Karan's death, neither took the throne. Strangely enough his son number one, Mahap goes off, not too far off mind you, to Dungarpur and forms his own kingdom, the Dun kingdom- a kingdom within a kingdom. Son number two, Rahap, tries to find a kingdom for himself too and goes to Sisodia to pester the Ruler there, Rana[15] Mokal of Mandore whom he defeats, and not only takes the title, the city, but also the name of that city, Sisodia, thus forming his own Dynasty of that name- after all kingdoms come and go, but names stick for ever. Son number three, and it is not clear if he was a younger son, or if he was adopted as heir since Karan was left without any sons after they had run off to meet other destinies which makes one presume disputes were in abundance. Whatever be the case, son number three, Kshem sits on the throne of Mewar at Ahar until 1172 when his successor has to relocate the capital at the same abode of son number one- Dungarpur which remained the capital while one state after another fell under the conquest of the Muslim Mahon of Ghur. This of course includes Gujarat which together with Mewar had always been a favourite prey for the invaders.

But for the invaders, Delhi was the main target, because it acted as buffer between the aggressor and the rest of India; so in 1192 Mohammed from Ghur,[16] having conquered a base in Punjab, plunges unto Delhi and completely devastates the Rajput confederacy which had mustered together all their forces without a single exception. It was not a pretty sight. More than one hundred and fifty Rajput Sovereigns had rallied around the Chauhan[17] Rajput Ruler of Delhi Prithviraj III, and the ultimate best of the Rajputs were without a sign of mercy, massacred. Rawal Mathan who had succeeded to the throne of Mewar that same year was one of the few

15 King
16 144 km. From north of Kabul
17 One of the four Rajput dynasties (the other three are: Pratiharas, Paramaras and Solankis)

who had managed to come out alive even though there was little left to live for after such sheer devastation.

The Ruler of Delhi Prithviraj III was captured and brutally executed sending his severed head rolling down rocks and crevices to the anguished Rajput forces bleeding to death below. All this was done in the name of religion. Islam had decreed that all should be converted or face the sword. Not a happy alternative for many of the beings that made up what is otherwise called humanity. But the irony was that most of the world, as it was at that time, had already fallen under the Islam sword- the Middle East, Africa, Spain and now India. And to spite it all the campaign of conversion included the destruction of the libraries of Alexandria and Damascus, creating darkness where there was light, at least considered so by less common mortals of other beliefs, but none the less still pertaining to that mass of flesh and blood called humanity.

Thus not only was the best Rajput blood spilt to stop the surge of this oppression but the aggressor made sure that the least sign that pertained or reminded of a Rajput existence from the present or the past, if it was made of substance and matter, if it was tangible, would be no more-wrecked, destroyed, burnt anything so that no breath of the Hindu gods could breathe evermore upon their disciples and be forever blind to their suffering. However, not all was the invader able to destroy, what is and was intangible could neither be touched and even less destroyed- that is why the spirit, belief and the being of a Rajput was not and could not be silenced. Hence, from here- with, rising from these barbarous ashes, Mewar Kings pledged themselves from now and the future to defend the life as decreed to them by nature than to fall into the slavery of the aggressor- this, was promised at the final battle of Tarain[18] in 1192. And this pledge, can be seen being unfolded, in some cases decidedly better than in others, throughout the length of time, and through whichever Ruler alternated as Trustee of Mewar.

---

18   16 km N.W. of Delhi

CHAPTER FOUR

Light Is Plunged Into Darkness

Muslim control over India; eight years 1253-1261 are lost from Mewar's history; Shah Ala-ud-dinkhil sets his eye on Padamini, wife to Mewar's 42nd Ruler, Ratan, causing the 1st Sack of Chittor 1303

Mohammed of Ghur was now the indisputable Ruler of Delhi and in order to distinguish himself from previous dominions, created the Delhi Sultanate with himself the Sultan. By the year 1206 when the said Sultan leaves this terrain world either by known or unknown hands, being succeeded by his slave Aibak, hence The Slave Dynasty; Mohammed of Ghur had captured and placed under his control all the states in Northern India, except for one, Mewar.

Mewar standing ice bright and alone among a constellation of falling stars watched almost powerless as the new Sultan Iltutmish destroyed the then capital of Mewar, Nagda, with the aim of forcing the 39th Ruler of Mewar, Jaitra Singh to succumb to Islam. But Jaitra had other plans. Wiping the dust from his feet and his breast as one who had fallen and engulfed in the sand, he marched upon Chittor, which by then had been taken by Malwa from the fallen Solanki Ruler in Gujarat. However, Malwa, in turn had been conquered by the Sultan Itutmish and, perhaps not as spectacularly as his predecessor Bappa Rawal did, but nevertheless as determinedly, Jaitra secured the fortress for Mewar which he immediately proceeded to make the capital of the Kingdom once more.

However, Jaitra does not leave things at that. Knowing that the Sultan would by no means allow Mewar to keep their fortress, indeed even their independence, within a few decades the Ruler of Mewar managed to put a stop to Iltumish's intentions of proceeding south or to wipe out as many Rajput hold-outs that stood in his way of conquering India. Even though

Iltumish's existence on this earth had come to an end by 1236, the Muslim control on India had not lost its hold because by 1253 when also Jaitra of Mewar is no more- the throne of Mewar remains empty for at least eight years, which for any kingdom is a mighty long time to be without a Ruler. Not a trace remains of that rent in the woven textile of Mewar's history, it simply remains a space covered up by darkness which no one wants to tear away and remember. So be it, let these eight years be lost in the darkness of forgetfulness.

But it was to get darker even further as the darkness had not yet begun. The years that followed, towards the middle of the 13th century, saw the end of the Solanki dynasty in Gujarat, prey to their Feudatories, the Vaghlea chiefs of Dholka. The Paramara Rajputs in Malwa manage to keep their independence for half a century longer than their counterparts in Gujart while the Jhalawads founded by Harpaldeva in the north east of Gujarat, not being such a powerful dynasty, seemed to have been ignored, the aggressor probably thought they were not worth the catch as there were much more big fish available but for the hunting.

In the meantime the Slave Dynasty had run dry of successors and were replaced by the Khil Ji Dynasty, so as to be distinguished from their predecessors the Sultans, they called themselves "Shah". The first Shah, Firoz, came to the throne in 1290 and only stayed six years, the second, Ibrahim I did not complete the year in which Firoz was taken to the next world, presumably, and he in turn was quickly replaced by one called Ala-ud-din who for those not of the area is better expressed as Aladdin, having nothing to do of course with the gene of the lamp that is so well known by all in the, by comparison more sombre, Western world.

Shah Ala-ud-din Khil Ji, to give his full name, although to add 'Sultan' is also in keeping; is worth a special mention, if only for the damage he had caused. The first to fall under his steel is Mewar's greatest alley and the original homeland of Mewar's Guhilot Dynasty, Gujarat. Even though Gujarat had put up an immense defence, nevertheless, after a year of continuous slaughter, by 1298, the deed was done. The Shah's roving eye next fell on Padmini a native of Ceylon, although this name is totally invented by the writer who told the story two hundred years later, nevertheless, Padamini, was one of the Ranis[19] of the 42nd Ruler of Mewar, Ratan Singh, consequently, the Princess from Ceylon was Ratan's wife. However, The Sultan may have had a roving eye, but see Padmini, he could not, as the only males that were allowed to gaze on wives were close

19 Queen

relatives or the husband himself. Nevertheless, Ala-ud-din was determined to see her. However one cannot but think that the reason for this stubborn determination was not totally due to Padamini's renown beauty but most likely because, to see the Mewar's Ruler's Rani, not only by a male who is a stranger but the enemy too would be the ultimate violation against Rajput honour, hence, Ala-ud-in persisted. However, in Padamini, Ala-ud-in had met his match.

So as not to be the cause of a pretext for Ala-ud-in to invade Mewar with all the forces he was able to gather from a large slice of India, when things started going wrong, Padamini put her plan into action- with all due credit, she was not just a pretty face. Unfortunately, her husband, Ratan, was not as enlightened as she was who, in order to put a stop to the Sultan's aggression which persisted throughout the year of 1302, he had promised the Sultan could view Padamini's reflection in the pool outside her quarters, and that would have to do, in exchange of course for a cease fire. Ala-ud-din accepted, if that was all that was on offer. At the conclusion of the view of the reflection upon which the Sultan offered many compliments on the beauty he had just chanced to admire, Ratan escorted his 'guest' to the gate but before he could close the immense wooden portals Ala-ud-din's soldiers grabbed the Mewar Ruler and dragged him away as a ransom in exchange for Padamini, and this time the Sultan demanded the real thing, no reflections or other ephemeral, elusive nonsense either.

Thus, having to take matters into her own hands, Padamini sent word diplomatically expressed, so as not to place the Sultan too much on the defensive, that she would agree to exchange herself with her husband so that Mewar would regain their rightful Ruler. But to alleviate her sudden departure, and be of a more cheerful disposition thus enabling him to make his ravaging, when the moment came, much more succulent, she would like him to consent to allow her to be accompanied by her own personal maidens of which they numbered over seven hundred in all. The Sultan did not hesitate for an instant to fulfil any request Padamini made, his mind was solely besotted in ravishing Padamini as soon as possible and of course there was no intention of letting Mewar see their Ruler ever again, Ratan had his days on this earth counted. Ala-ud-din may have been quite right in underestimating Ratan or rather Ratan had been foolish enough to have trusted the enemy and consequently the Sultan was lying back waiting for the fruit to simply fall into his hands unaware of what Rajput women could be capable of and of which Padamini was to be an example that would shine in the whatever historical annals would be available for future generations to peruse.

Overnight, the Queen arranged for a procession of palanquins, each being carried by six slaves which were Rajput soldiers in disguise carrying indeed, not the retinue of maidens as she had expressed but well armed and the best of Rajput warriors of Mewar. Padamini's uncle, Gora, travelled in her palanquin for greater security since he was famed to have slaughtered any who stood in his way, back in Ceylon, where the family originated. Arriving at the Muslim camp which was below the fortress of Chittor, the procession stopped and Gora, disguised as Padamini which was not too difficult coming from a race where even males are of an nimble disposition and besides, his face was covered as was the custom for ladies, requested, in as an effeminate voice as he could modulate, to have one last interview alone with her husband Ratan before parting for ever. Ala-ud-din, of course, being so near to soon savour his juicy prey, could not deny 'Padamini' anything, therefore consented. The Queen's palanquin was taken to where the Mewar Ruler was kept prisoner and all soldiers were withdrawn. As soon as Gora released Ratan, Rajput warriors immediately sprang out from all palanquins, adding to the other warriors disguised as slaves and for an interminable moment, all hell seemed to have been let loose. In the pandemonium that ensued the bewildered Ala-ud-din realized that the object of his desire was no-where in sight and heavily gnawed by having been pulled by the leg, struck Gora and five hundred Rajputs to death, retreated back to Delhi with his much depleted army like a beaten dog with his tail between his legs.

This was however, the last moment of glory that Ratan and Padamini were allowed to savour for the wrath brought upon Ala-ud-din was immeasurable as he soon was to prove at the turn of the new year. In January 1303, Ala-ud-din marched upon the fortress with as many soldiers as to engulf the whole of Chittor. Seeing no hope of escape let alone victory, the women, in their thousands led by Padamini performed the first of the three most renown jauhur[20]in Mewar's history. The men putting on the saffron robes of death, charged to their death. Ala-ud-in entering the fortress as the victorious conqueror without the added bother of having to dispense of a husband, immediately went in search of the object of his desire, and this time, at last, there could be no escape. Although the price was high, life itself, Padamini did however, manage to outwit the Sultan

---

20   self-immolation: suicide by fire of Rajput women

in the end; for of the beautiful body he had thought to consummate his deed upon, found nothing but ashes in its place.

CHAPTER FIVE

The Guhilot Dynasty is Replaced by the Sisodian Dynasty

Ancestry of Rana Laskha from Sisodia; the fate of Malwa and Gujarat Rajputs; the Delhi dynasties; Hamir, becomes the first Sisodian Ruler and institutes the name "Maharana"; Hamir's successor Kshetra, his two illegitimate sons Mera and Cacha. Kshetra's successor Lakha, his marriage to his Crown Prince Choonda's intended; Choonda forfeits his primogeniture rights in favour of Mokal

Afther the massacre of Ratan Singh I and his royal family in January 1303, there was no single survivor of Mewar left in Chittor it could well be supposed that this was the end of the reign which all in all did not fare badly as the Guhilot Dynasty had survived well over seven hundred years whereas other dynasties including that of the Sultans survived barely two or three hundred years in all. But as it is a universally acknowledged fact that Mewar is the longest serving dynasty to date, something must have happened during this period of upheaval to ensure the continuance of the Royal line.

With Ala-ud-din and his armies outnumbering the Rajputs by far camped beneath the walls of Chittorgarh for lengths of time, in the much providential group of elders that counselled Ratan, Rana Laksha from Sisodia was well in the foreground. Indeed the whole of these events could well be looked upon as the gods taking the law into their own hands or as is otherwise known- Divine Justice- since Rana Laksha from Sisodia had probably more right to the throne of Mewar than Ratan had. Ratan was a successor of Kshem Singh who was the third son of Karan I, whereas Laksha was a successor of the first son, Rahap, who was therefore the Crown Prince but who for some reason or other had to leave the then capital Ahar and with his second brother seek other pastures, this being the city of Sisodia where Rahap founds the Sisodia family in the 1160s or thereabouts.

Hence the annihilation of Ratan's lineage could be looked upon as justice having taken its proper course placing back on the throne of Mewar the successor who would have been to Karan I in 1168 almost hundred and fifty years previously. Laksha with all of his ten sons had rallied in defence of Ratan at Chittor but when things started getting tight, the Sarders[21] decided the time had come to take measures in safeguarding the Mewar Lineage. Strange as it seems, there is no mention of Ratan's sons or heir to the throne but all is concentrated on Laksha and his sons. Eight of Laksha's sons remain in oblivion but two have made it to the chronicles, Ari and Ajay. Ari, the first born was Rana Laksha of Sisodia Crown Prince who in turn had a son still a minor named Hamir. Laksha ordered the infant Hamir to be taken by his uncle Ajay to safety which meant Kelwara in the vicinity of the Aravalli hills, while Laksha's Crown Prince Ari and the rest of his sons would stay and help Ratan face the enemy forever waiting in ambush below. While everyone's attention was centred on Padamini and Ala-ud-din's roving eye, to escape through Chittor's underground passages, was for the royal infant not too traumatic feat to achieve.

After the massacre by Ala-ud-din, the Sultan places his own son on the throne of Mewar but as can be imagined was not received with shouts of joy therefore the shrewd Ala-ud-din replaces his son with one of his already conquered Rajput vassal Rao[22] Maldeo. Whatever few numbers were left, the Rajput clans gathered around Ajay in Kelwara, who with his young nephew Hamir had escaped before the massacre at Chittor took place and thus began guerrilla attacks on the Imperial strongholds. In the early 1320s Ajay too dies in battle. Thus it was that when both the Sisodia lineage and the Guhilot lineage which in effect were one and of the same blood, had been slaughtered, the Sarders proclaimed the sole survivor of both families, Hamir of Sisodia, Ruler of Mewar, which the teenage Prince accepted most kindly but when he leaves exile and takes Chittor in 1326 he extended to his already inherited title of Rana, also Maha, in other words 'Great' which placed together to Rana is not interpreted as one would suppose 'Great King', that is reserved for the interpretation of the title of 'Maharajah' but 'Maharana' which gives him the title of 'King of Kings'.

---

21 Elders who advise the Ruler, safeguard and proclaim the new Ruler
22 Rathore Rajput King, in Marwar

Not only did Hamir change the title of the Ruler of Mewar but also the family name, since his great-grandfather Rahap who left the court of Mewar and his angry father Karen I in the 1160s, had changed his name from Guhilot to the name of the city he conquered, namely Sisodia. Hamir, having been proclaimed Ruler of Mewar founded the Sisodian Dynasty which both title and name has succeeded him ever since. It is also a small wonder that this, as he was, young Prince, having spent his entire life in exile little by little regains most of the provinces lost, thus making Chittor once more the great capital that it had been in the days that Bappa Rawal had first regained it for Mewar.

Hamir's neighbours, the Paramara Rajputs in Malwa and the Solanki Rajputs in Gujarat had not fared so well, since both being captured by the Delhi self proclaimed Sultan, Ala-ud-din, they remained under the power of the Delhi Sultanate for the rest of that century and neither did the outbreak of the Bubonic plague, better known as the Black death, deter in any way the Sultanate's hold on these two regions. This attitude was continued after the 2nd Khil Ji Dynasty, which had run out of heirs was replaced by the Tughluq and 3rd Dynasty which occupied the Sultanate throne in Delhi for the rest of that century. Curiously, each of the five dynasties which succeeded one another barely lasted over one hundred years each.

Hamir's days in the world ended in the year 1366 after a relative long reign of thirty-six years and was succeeded by Kshetra who although reigned for only half as much time managed to make a mark for Mewar both for better and for worse. The better part was that he regained the Rajput cities of Jaipur and Ajmer in the north west of Mewar and Mandalgarh with its strategic fortress in the south east. However, whatever glory he gained as a valiant Rajput was less laudable when it came to matters with the ladies as indeed a question of marriage had put an end to his days by unknown hands, nevertheless, not before having fathered two illegitimate offsprings namely Mera and Cacha who in turn create their own share of adversity as it will be unfolded in due time. It was his legitimate son however, Lakha, (not to be confused with his forefather, Laska) who succeeded the womanising Kshetra as 45th Ruler of Mewar and 3rd bearing the name of Sisodia.

Lakha regained all remaining cities in Mewar that his father had not managed to take back from the Delhi Sultan but being a valiant warrior was not the only talent at his disposal. He was a resourceful ruler, developing the Zawar mines bringing a not indifferent sum of income to

Mewar which enabled him to restore the damage to palaces, fortresses and temples that Ala-ud-din had caused with the construction of numbers of reservoirs and lakes not seen before. However the complication with women seemed to be a family habit that he also had inherited. Even though in all fairness it wasn't entirely Lakha's fault that in his old age the line of succession instead of flowing straight took a detour.

Had he not had a Crown Prince, Choonda, who happened to be picky as to whom he would marry and an ambitious neighbouring king of Marwar[23], the Rathore Rajput Rao Ranmal, who wanted to expand his alliances at all cost, Lakha may not have made such a blunder. When Rao Ranmal's ambassador carrying a coconut, as is the case when offering a lady in marriage, came to the court of Mewar, fortuitously, it happened that Lakha's Crown Prince was not at home and so his father accepted the present saying that his son would be honoured by the gift for certainly it was not meant for an old man like himself. The Maharana said what he said half jokingly but it would be quite legitimate to think that he half wished the young Rao Ranmal's sister, who was on offer, was indeed intended for an old man like himself. On his return Choonda refused point blank to marry the damsel saying he could not marry the lady his father had made fun of which is doubtful that this should be the real reason. Most probable it was because Princess Hansabai was not to the Crown Prince liking or perhaps, since it was reputed that Choonda was a dutiful son, sensed his father wanted her himself and obliged him on the matter. However, whatever the reason, it was so rooted and strong enough that when Mokal, Lakha's son with the young Marwar Princess was born, the Maharana made Choonda promise to give up his birthright of primogenitor in favour of his step-brother. Choonda swore this promise and his father made him Regent to Mokal should Lakha die before the infant, Crown Prince, became of age.

When Maharana Lakha is killed in battle in 1421, Choonda carried out his promise faithfully and acted as a worthy Regent for Mokal who was merely 5 years old. However, the Rajmata[24] Hansabai, feeling that she was losing her grip on power at court and of course, spurned by her relatives in Marwar accused Choonda of plotting to regain his title of Maharana which was hardly the case, but choonda, rather than having to continue bickering with the woman that once he had the courage to spurn and telling Hansabai that if she was Rajmata it was only thanks

---

23 Not to be confused with the Kingdom of Mewar
24 Queen Mother

to him anyway, packed his bags and made his abode in Mandu, capital of Malwa. No sooner had he left than a storm of Rathores from Marwar fell upon the neighbouring Chittor with the sole intent of possessing the throne of Mewar which was timely thwarted by the murder of Maharana Mokal at the age of twenty four. This however did not help matters because Mokal had a son Kumbha, a fact that could not be ignored. However the assassins of Mokal did not, of course, deem the death of Mokal as an obstacle to obtaining the throne since they considered to have been on equal footing to obtaining the throne of Mewar as their late step-brother, Lakha. Indeed, the murderers and Lakha were all fathered by Kshetra, the 44th Maharana, the only difference was that Lakha was the legitimate Crown Prince and his two half-brothers Chacha and Mera were the issue of Keshetra's concubine, and this, the murder of Mokal was their revenge for being considered illegitimate.

Mokal's son Kumbha takes the throne of Mewar at the age of six while his grandmother calls upon her relations at Marwar to put an end to Chacha and Mera who had in the meantime fled to a fortress in the mountains of Pali capturing a virgin on the way infuriating the father who set on the track of his daughter and timely informed the Marwar soldiers who surely and promptly put a final end to the malevolent pair and securing the virgin safely back to her father's arms, whether intact or not however, remains unknown. As soon as the infant Kumbha takes the throne his grandmother's brother Rao Ranmal gets rid of Choonda's younger brother Rghudeo who was far too near the throne for the comfort of the Marwar Ruler and ironic as it may seem the grandmother Hansabai possibly sensing that as Regent she too was an obstacle for her brother, calls upon the man who once refused to marry her, Choonda, for protection, who timely arranges for Kumbha, his nurse and grandmother to disguise themselves at a religious festival whilst he marches on Chittor with a small army and happily puts an end to Rao Ranmal and the rest of the Marwar Rathors camped there- indeed it was a happily enough event, for the Marwar Ruler was quite under the influence of opium at the time. His son Jodha, however, manages to save himself and goes on to found a city of his own, Jodhpur, thus keeping his hands off Chittor evermore.

And Choonda is true to his word maintaining the oath made to his father of not taking the throne of Mewar, which at this point he could easily have done so. One cannot help express some admiration for this character who ought to have been, but never was, King of Kings.

CHAPTER SIX

The Jhalawad Rajputs in Gujarat

1400s- Jhalawhad Ruler at odds with Rathores; at war with Sultan of Gujarat; Wagho Ji and the disaster of Kuwa; his successor Rajodhar founds Halward; Raimal's (Mewar) ancestry

From the reign of Lakha in 1382 to that of his grandson Kumbha in 1433, fifty one conflicting years elapsed but Mewar was not the only throne to be at odds with the Marwar Rathores north east of Mewar; the Ruler of the relative younger state, the south west neighbouring Jhalawad, in Gujarat, had more than one warring Rathore to face.

Somewhere around the time of Lakha's reign and most likely not after 1411 the 17th Ruler descendent from the founder[25] of Jhalawad, was Ranmal Ji, who, for some reason or other, the Rathores of Barmar-Kotda attacked and perfidiously murdered him which did not go down well with his son and successor Satatsal Ji who, having to leave Halvad, made his capital, at Mandal and revenged his father by ploughing up the Rathores's villages with donkeys. That, if anything spurred the Rathores to leave him alone. But ploughing up the Rathores' villages was not the only strategy Satasal Ji was to put into action. He was also forced to battle against Ahmed Shah, who being the Sultan of Gujarat was super keen to be rid of minor kingdoms that stood in his way from the claim of sole Ruler of the whole of Gujarat.

Considering that the Sultan named the capital of Gujarat Ahmedabad, after himself, it is no wonder that he had not planned to have this Makwana survivor clutter up his territory. Three times Satasal Ji had to prevent the Sultan from taking his kingdom and in doing so the Rajput did not employ simple donkeys which meant that every time a battle occurred Satasal

---

25 Harpaldeva 1090-1130

Ji was left with less resources than he had before, however, at the same time he managed to get rid of the Rathores and regained Jhalawad, for his son Jet Singh Ji because the time for Satasal Ji to surrender his soul to the heavens in 1420, or thereabouts, had come. Unfortunately, Jet Singh Ji, during his long reign, had not been able to stave off Ahmed Shah, or the other Sultans that came after him. Hence, at his death, depleted and defeated the Jhala Rajput family had to abandon Patdi in Jhalawad and move to Kuwa.

In 1469, Wagho Ji replaces his father as Ruler in Kuwa. Wagho Ji in effect is not the Crown Prince, not even the second son but the third. However there is no sign of this having been a take over bid on behalf of Wagho Ji, with all the battles that this Jhala Rajput family had to face, he was one of the few surviving sons left. It was said that Wagho Ji was rebellious as he would not accept the Sultan's dominion, that itself seems a colossal miscarriage of justice that Wagho Ji should go down in history as rebellious- it is to be questioned as to which ruler would have just stood by and allowed another to take over one's kith, kin, religion, pots and pans to boot! Anyway, history claims that because Wagho Ji was rebellious made the son of the Sultan of Gujarat, Prince Khali Khan, later Muzaffar Shah, attack him. The battle took place at Sadipur and going beyond every aspiration, the Rajput won.

The Muslim Prince retreated to the safety of his father's capital, Ahmedabad claiming that no one had the power to put in position of inferiority the son of a Sultan and since Wagho Ji succeeded in doing so, every Rajput in the land had to taste the end of a Muslim sword, in other words Gujarat had to be rid of these miserable infidels- an opinion not shared by those concerned by any means. Hence Mahmud Shah musters together an immense army and marched upon the Jhala's capital Kuwa. When Wagho Ji sees that his relative small city is completely swamped by Muslim soldiers who had turned out in their thousands to avenge their Prince's honour, knew he had to take one of the two options available to him, be slain or starve to death- none of which, he thought, was apt for him. He therefore decided to persuade the enemy that he was still there when he wasn't. Before leaving however, he instructed his Ranis[26] that while he was out there on the battlefield, should his banner fall which would be the sign that he had passed to a better life, they would put themselves on the funeral pyre, making sure of constructing one first in case of the need for its use arose.

---

26 Queens

Fighting with his Rajput soldiers as he had never fought in his entire life, Wagho Ji managed to regain Kuwa, the Jhala capital. But exhausted as they all were, the standard bearer not having slept for a week, collapsed to the ground in fatigue with the banner on top of him and slept. The Ranis who were always on a look out from the fortress above the city not seeing the banner flying for several hours thought the worst, but not having prepared the funeral pyre, as they had sinned of optimism, decided to do the next best thing and threw themselves down a well inside the palace walls. When Wagho Ji returned to the Palace and saw that he had been bereft of all his conjugal affections decided that life wasn't worth living and went back unto the field and thrust himself into battle so completely that he refused to leave the field until he and his Sarders[27] were accurately slain in true Rajput style. This meant that the Mahmudeons were victorious and captured the Jhala capital which was so destroyed that it never was a capital for anyone anymore and would have disappeared into oblivion were it not for the fact that it remains memorable among the Jhalas as Kuwa-no-ker, in other words, a great cock-up for anything that goes wrong.

If Wagho Ji was third in line to the throne, his successor, Rajodhar Ji was eighth, the others having all been massacred at Kuwa. At this point in his life, Rajodhar Ji had no father and of course, no mother; but he also had no Palace or land to build one on- in fact he had nothing. But Rajodhar did not lose heart and while out hunting, (he had to get food, somehow), saw a hare. Usually hares scarper as fast as you can see them, but this one didn't. It stood on its hind legs, right in front of Rajodhar's horse and confronted it. Rajodhar was taken quite aback by the audaciousness of this extraordinary creature and decided that this was the spot where his new kingdom would arise. Thus, in 1488, as the foundations for the Palace were laid, the town of Halward or Dhrangadhara as it later came to be known.

Rajodhar Ji was not as prolific as his father and only had three sons from just two Ranis. For a man without a kingdom, it was not easy to find a wife but he did get one from the Chief of the Rathores in Idar in Gujarat, which were not the same Rathores as those in Marwar, that his grandfather, Satarsal, had invaded with his donkeys at the beginning of the century. Idar Rathores were the ones who were also friendly with the Maharana, as the Sisodian Ruler Raimal of Mewar at the time was called.

Raimal's father was Kumbha, the great Kumbha as he was later known and it was no exaggeration for he was not only a remarkable sovereign,

---

27 Chieftains

warrior, engineer and constructor but he was also a gifted writer, poet, playwright and artist. Unfortunately he was greatly influenced by fortune tellers and sent his Crown Prince Raimal into exile to Idar because it had been predicted that he was the Marahana was to die soon and he thought it was because his son was eager to sit on the throne. The death of Kumbha had been predictely timely enough only it wasn't by the hands of his Crown Prince Raimal but by his younger son Udai who killing his father usurped the throne from his elder brother Raimal in 1468 and was to remain for five years, only time enough for Raimal to organize himself and take the throne which was rightfully his. Strangely enough, it is said, Udai was conveniently struck by lightning thus putting an end to his days on this earth one day in 1473.

"Now, there's a lucky man…" Rajodhar said to his Idar wife, one day. "His brother Udai being struck down by lightning, just like that, leaving the throne quite empty for Raimal to sit on it," she said as she sieved the flour onto the chapatti,[28] "and is still sitting on it."

"How can you say how things really went, it was twenty years ago… the Elders of the times have very feeble memories now. Besides, are you not forgetting Raimal is the rightful heir, and not Udai?" He pulled down his sword and inspected the edge. "Being Primogenitor not always is a guarantee that you get the throne- look at my case, I was the eighth son."

"Because the others are dead in battle, and those who aren't have gone to other kingdoms… There'll be a Jhala clan in Tana soon, which is a security for our two sons." The Idar wife glanced over to the other side of the room where Ajja, a bit taller than Sajja were gaming with sticks as Rajputs would with swords.

"Let's hope Ajja and Sajja never have need of relations…" he said thoughtfully, "Look at the Mewar throne!"

"Which event in particular are you referring to, husband? To the one twenty years ago when Udai kills his father Kumbha, or shall we start at the beginning of the Sisodia clan?" The Idar wife stopped and smiled gingerly, "No, let's go even further back, back to the last Guhilot."

"Ratan? That freak! What an inglorious end to a noble line"

"Inglorious!" The Idar Rani huffed. "If you did half as much for me as he did for his Padmini, I would more than gladly throw myself on a funeral pyre with you," she smiled provocatively.

---

28   A sort of pancake made of bread

"You will throw yourself on a funeral pyre with me anyway!" Rajodhar retorted.

"It's another thing if you do it willingly," she sighed. He looked at his wife menacingly.

"No other man is going to dip his chappati, in my dish!"

"It certainly is only dipping," she moaned to herself shifting the round chapatti disk from one hand to the other to shape it, "only two sons!" Then looking at her husband curiously, she added, "why do you insist on calling Ratan a freak, after all he did prevent Ala-ud-Din get his paws on that beautiful creature, Padmini?"

"How could Ratan have possibly believed that a foreigner would have kept his word?" Rajodhar cut the air with his sword indignantly. "Ratan gives high ranking hospitality to the Sultan and how does the Sultan pay his host back?"

"By asking to add Padmini to his harem."

"See, what I mean?" He swished his sword in the air once more. "Brass faced he was that Ala-ud-Din. He had already collected enough Rajput Ranis."

"But Padmini was something else... That, is what happens when Rajas marry exceptionally beautiful women- they get into trouble." She eyed her husband with intent.

"No fear of that happening to me," Rajodhar said insufferably. His wife squinted her eyes and pouted her lips,

"I may be no Padmini, but you are no Ratan either!" Her husband shrugged his shoulders. "Ratan acted nobly, as a true Rajput," she huffed.

"I would think twice before escorting a Sultan to the gate after he has asked for my Rani to be added to his harem," feeling his sword between his hands. His wife smiled coquettishly.

"Really?" she sighed.

"Now, don't get any ideas, no Sultan is going to be asking for you..." His wife pouted disagreeably. "As far as I'm concerned Padmini was the one with the brains, not Ratan," he concluded.

"There wasn't much he could do after being captured at his own gate-way and taken off, now was there?"

"Still, it was Padmini who schemed up the idea of setting off to the Sultan's Palace with seven hundred Rajputs dressed up as ladies-in-waiting and freed Ratan. She, on the other hand," Rajodhar slid his finger around his silky black moustache, "did not just sit there..."

"Do you really think it's true?"

"That she would agree to go to the Sultan in exchange for Ratan's freedom?"

"No, not that," his wife said energetically, "Did she really convince the Sultan to let her take all seven hundred of her ladies in waiting?"

"The Sultan was so greedy that he couldn't wait to get her hands on her- and her seven hundred maids- had they been maids, of course," Rajodhar said as he laughed with pleasure. "Indeed, they were Rajputs, all seven hundred of them!"

"That's something, isn't it... Persuading a Rajput to dress up as a woman!"

"A Rajput will do this and more for his Ruler."

"A neat little trick which stopped that scheming Sultan getting his hand on Ratan's Rani."

"But it didn't stop Ratan from getting slain." Rajodhar's black eyes peered from his bearded face. "Just one year later... Ratan- the last of the Guhilots - reigned, one solitary, single year- to the Bhadon[29] of 1303- almost two hundred years ago."

"So, the Sultan did take his revenge."

"That Prat!" Rajodhar cried as he slipped his sword back in its sheath. "Thousands dead. Not even the Paramaras, our neighbours, did he spare..."

"And the women of course, all on the funeral pyre."

"Women, children, thousands of them too, led by Padmini dressed in her bridal gown, went down to the cellars where the pyre was erected. That, jauhar,[30] when Mewar lost Chittor, was the only and greatest jauhar ever known.

"There's one good thing, if you allow me to say so husband; it pleases me no end that ..." the blood was steadily rising in her cheeks, "that viper wasn't able to get his hands on Padmini after all that."

"He certainly came too late. When he saw the smoke of the women and children, even before he entered the fort, he was so enraged that he massacred every single living being in sight- more than thirty thousand- it is said."

---

29 August/September Hindu months
30 Self immolation by fire

CHAPTER SEVEN

The Rajputs Of Jhalawad Lose Their Throne

Rajodhar's sons Ajja, Sajja and their usurper stepbrother; Ajja and Sajja seek refuge at the court of Raimal- Mewar

"So, with the end of Chittor, that was the end of the Guhilot dystany too."

"Yes, but not the end of the Ghadi[31] of Mewar…"

"All Ratan's children were massacred!"

"Thirty years before Ratan came to the Ghadi, his predecessor Karen had a son called Rahap who set up a dynasty of his own, known as Sisodia."

"Isn't that what the Maharana of Mewar is now called, Raimal of Sisodia?" The Idar wife paused and bending her head sideways to follow the movement of her hands continued, "Obviously, after Ratan's death there was no one on the throne of Mewar in Chittor since the capital had been taken by Ala-ud-Din."

"There was someone on the throne, but it wasn't one of the Mewar dynasty, but Ala-ud-Din's son, a foreigner."

"But Raimal is now back on the throne in Chittor, how did Chittor return to Mewar?"

"The other part of the Guhilot family, the Sisodians, managed to save themselves by going in exile to Kelwara. Hence twenty two years later, and more slaughter, Hamir, Rana Laska Sisodia's teenage grandson finally overcomes the Muslims and takes Chittor once more."

---

31 Throne

"Why didn't Rana Laska's son take the Ghadi instead of putting a teenager on the throne."

"Who? Ari? Couldn't oblige, was slaughtered in battle."

"Doesn't it seem odd to put a mere teenager on the Ghadi... I wouldn't like Ajja to..."

"No chance, I'm healthy, strong... I'm not going to die yet, besides Maharana Mokal and his son the Great Kumbha were only five or six..."

"I can see why Mokal was so young, his father Laska..."

"Lakha," Rajodhar corrected, "Mokal's father was Lakha, without the s. Laska, with the s, was the grandfather of Hamir, the first Sisodian to take the throne of Mewar, and he lived at the beginning of the last century not at the end as Lakha did."

"Lakha or Laska whatever it is... these names are all so confusing. Anyway, it all boils down to me wanting to say that Mokal's father should have been ashamed of himself!" The Idar wife slammed more dough on the board as Rajodhar leaned back with laughter. "Fancy marrying that Rathore girl who was to have married his son, Choonda, instead!"

"But Choonda did not want to marry her!" he said still laughing. "So, what could old Lakha do, but marry her himself."

"And the girl's father, that Rathore, let Lakha marry her, at his age?"

"The girl didn't have a father, but a brother, Rao Ranmal, King of Marwar- note Marwar with an 'a'- on the northern border of Mewar, Jodhpur to be precise."

"Never mind that. I want to know if this brother of hers... that Rao Ranmal, or whoever it was, actually let the young girl marry such an old man- Maharana or no Maharana."

"Only on condition that Lakha would proclaim the male issue from this marriage as Lakha's heir... which is precisely what happened with young Mokal."

"See what I mean, the Rathore king wasn't so keen in the marriage at all- It was Lakha who wanted to marry the girl. Dirty old viper!"

"I thought that was an expression you used only for Muslims?" picked up his goblet with his left hand. "You mustn't be so hard on Lakha. He only wanted an alliance with the King of Marwar, not another war."

"I bet," the Idar wife said, not convinced.

"What if I tell you that Lakha was not interested in the girl at all, but it was the Rathore King that wanted to get his hands on the throne of Mewar... besides, there was always the question of covering up for an erring Crown Prince Choonda."

"No one cares a hoot as to who wants to marry who."

"Of course, why should that surprise you?"

"Somehow, it doesn't seem fair- I mean no one dared stop Ratan marrying his beauty, even though she was not of royal blood."

"But he's a man."

"So? That's what I mean, it isn't fair, a man can choose, but a woman..."

"You married me because your father told you to, didn't you?"

"That's different."

"I don't see how."

"I wanted to marry you! You had guts, you built Halvad- there isn't a palace as magnificent as this..."

"Ah! So you married me for my wealth!" Rajodhar chided.

"Partly," his wife toyed, "and partly because you were a Rajput, a warrior, those muscles looked so manly!"

"It's time I took another Rani," Rajodhar huffed as he rose to leave.

"I suppose, I could do with some help around the house," the Idar wife muttered as she collected the crocks.

And so it happened. The Idar wife having seen more than thirty Springs was quite old and Rajodhar only having two sons, Ajja and Sajja, thought it best to supply fresh blood to the throne of Halvad. As the times were, two sons were barely enough to ensure continuity to the line of succession. His was a line of kings as Kesardeva, the Makwana, had promised his son Harpalveda that he would father a line of royal Rajput kings. And Rajodhar felt it was his duty to safeguard this by marrying a young girl from the neighbouring Paramaras.

In consequence, a son was born to the Paramara Rani and named Rano Ji. Towards the end of the 15th Century, the Idar wife dies and Rajodhar himself falls ill. It is only a melancholy sickness, for the loss of his Idar wife, nothing more, yet the father of his last wife, Laghdhir Ji hastens to come to the court of Halvard enquiring on the health of his son-in-law. As fate would have it, or fate being guided by a fatherly hand, it occurs that Rajodhar dies shortly after this ill-fated visit of his father-in-law. And while Rajodhar's two elder sons by his Idar wife, Ajja and Sajja join their father's funeral procession, Laghdhir Ji, manages by furtive and intense scheming with the principal Sardars to proclaim the Paramara's wife, nonetheless, his own grandson, heir to the throne of Halvard.

On their return, Ajja and Sajja were none too pleased about the matter. Ajja, with the aid of Sajja vainly tried to topple the young Rano Ji from the Ghadi and thence sit himself upon it, but a wild scramble came about and the numbers of the two brothers' alliance being few, were overcome by the others who were well reinforced by Paramara warriors, specially imported for the occasion. Ajja and Sajja thus resolved, even though not too willingly, to enlist the aid of, heaven forbid, the Amendabad Sultan. Taking advantage of the two brothers' absence, Laghdhir Ji did not stay there with his hands idly under his turban but with the offering of a Nazrana[32] consisting of a substantial number of coins in the right direction procured the legality of his grandson's succession. Thus once the successor had been properly anointed, the seal of his ordination could not be shattered and he remains king until death. Ajja and Sajja not wishing to tempt fate and inducing a malediction upon their heads by procuring the death of an anointed king, resolved to find another solution in exile.

Certainly, had Harpalveda been alive he would have been ill pleased by these events as the promise that he would father a line of rightful kings, at this stage in time with someone jumping the queue, seemed quite remote. Similarly, had the Idar Rani been here, considering that her native land, Idar, was the capital of the first Ruler of Mewar, Rawal Guhil, she would have stormed the Throne of Mewar for assistance. In good faith, the two brothers, first went to their mother's homeland, Idar, then to Jodhpur, but been coolly received in both places as there are always more rulers than thrones to accommodate them, the brothers decided to look elsewhere. However, from above, the Idar Rani must have guided her sons since they found acceptance and service at the Court of Maharana Raimal of Mewar.

Should anyone enquire on how Rano Ji fared, let it be known that he did not fare well. Once on the throne, and having being taught by an astute teacher as his maternal grandfather was, Rano Ji ordered the death of the father of a certain Malik Bakhan, who in turn, revenged his father by slaughtering Rano Ji, and this time there are no misgivings in slaying an anointed king... but then Mr Bakham junior was no Rajput and such matters were to him of no consequence. Having said the above, it is well to remember that Rajputs have murdered anointed kings; indeed Mokal, Lakha's third son was murdered by his uncles. Mokal's son the Great Kumbha who inherited the throne when barely ten years old was slain by his third son Udai. Udai was more fortunate, a thunderbolt of lightning struck him while on his horse, or so the locals say. And hence the Crown

---

32 Gift

Prince, Raimal, the legitimate heir of his father's throne, finally sits on the Ghadi.

Therefore, Raimal, sensitive to the deprivation of the right of Primogenitor having had first hand experience of that personally, welcomed Ajja and Sajja to his court warmly: while Ajja and Sajja being Jhala Rajputs could find no better mission in life than being at the service in the defence of their Lord. Contentment on all sides... now to war.

CHAPTER EIGHT

The Jhalawad Rajputs at the Court of Raimal Mewar 1473

Ajja and Sajja at the service of Mewar; warfare talk; Raimal and his sons Prithvi, Jaimal and Sangram

Kumbhalgarh, whose boundary wall is wide enough for eight horses to ride abreast and stretches through the ruggedness of the Arvalli Hills for 36 kilometres, is so impressive and forbidding a fortress that no Muslim had yet dared to assail its heights. And this is where we find Raimal licking his wounds after another assault from the Sultan of Malwa, Ghiyas-ud-Din. "Did you see that Ajja…" Raimal said hopping around on the only sound leg he had left. "Did you see how that son of a hog ran from the Suraj Pol[33] as soon as he saw me arrive?"

"'Tis no wonder Sire, you ran the full length of your blade through his left shoulder!"

"Ach!" Raimal groaned, angry with himself. "I should have aimed lower as he did."

"Be appeased Sire, Ghiyas-ud-Din's cries could be heard right to the bottom of Chittorgarh." Ajja said encouraging. "He is in a worse state than you, I should not wonder."

"Ach! This leg… tis only a scratch, in three noons and I'll be back on the field." Raimal looked around him stealthily, "but this time we must really win- no half measures, no half shoulders! I don't want that Muslim Hog on my doorstep again!"

"You mean on your gateway, Sire, don't you?" Sajja corrected as he joined them.

---

33 The name of one of the entrances to Kumbhalgarh

"Don't talk to me about Muslims on gateways," Raimal said referring to his not so prudent ancestor Ratan and his Padamini.

"They bank on surprise, sneaking up on us at the old Eastern Gate, thinking since your father Sire, the Great Kumbha having built seven other gates, Suraj Pol would be deserted."

"True!" Raimal answered standing deep in thought in front of a pile of bolsters thrown haphazardly on the floor. "Those sons of mine, always fighting," he muttered to himself "can't keep anything straight in this Rawala.[34]" With his bare foot hanging from his bandaged leg Raimal kicked a purple pillow to his right towards East, "This is Malwa," he said sticking his lance on top of the pillow as if butchering it, "where that Ghiyas-ud-Din Hog comes from." Next to it, to the North West, Raimal kicked an orange bolster, "And this is Chittor... You see why that Hog is always hovering round Chittor, he can't stand being so close..."

"And so far apart..." Ajja said with a laugh.

"He can't get used to Chittor being the capital of Mewar, although it was two hundred years ago that it was recaptured by my ancestors." Raimal said shaking his head.

"My father told me Chittor has always been the capital of Mewar," Sajja said. "I even remember him telling us when kids that Harpel the founder ..." he paused, "of our dynasty..."

"Which is no longer ours," his brother interrupted, "but no more of that now."

"Harpel aided Solanki of Gujarat to take Chittor from the then King of Malwa," Sajja continued as if to remind the Maharana of the ties that existed between the two dynasties, "in days when Rajputs were still Rajputs and head of their kingdoms."

"Chittor belongs to Mewar from times eternal," Raimal cried. "Bappa Rawal founded the Mewar Dynasty in Chittor more than seven hundred years ago- Malwa has always wanted to put their thumb on it..."

"Is it any wonder," Sajja said rubbing his bearded chin, as his father would have done back in Halvad. "since their ancestor Maun Mori built it."

"On Mewar's land! That's where that Malwa Mori built Chittor," Raimal objected forcibly, "it would be a wonder if Bappa Rawal didn't go and claim it! But now Chittor has been regained and it will remain, must remain in Mewar's hands!" Raimal thrust the lance into the purple bolster. "Plunderers, that's all they are..." The Maharana's eyes began to

---

34 Royal House

twinkle, "What did you just say Sajja? Surprise them... yes, we will play at their game... "

"My Lord?" Sajja enquired not having understood.

"We will surprise them!" Ramail concluded his outburst by slapping his hand heavily on Sajja's back. He beckoned Ajja to come near. "They think they are quite safe while we are barricaded in here."

"Indeed Sire," Ajja said, "But in that case, there's hardly any case in tarring here longer otherwise we are not foiling them in any way..."

"Do you think I'm a complete idiot?" the Maharana said gamely.

"We must leave Kumbhalgarh... but to where?" Ajja continued heedless of the jestful rebuke.

"Mandalgarh!" Raimal said slapping Ajja's back with a thrust of enthusiasm not realizing he had only one royal foot to stand on and practically stumbled over his lance were it not that Sajja had the good sense to place his shoulder under the Maharaja's armpit and Ajja quickly following suit prevented the poor man from provoking further injuries to himself.

The trick worked. While Ghiyas-ud-Din was licking his wounds somewhere in the North East of Marwar and thinking Raimal was doing the same thing in Kumbhalgarh, the Maharana, his five sons together with Ajja and Sajja had managed in just a week or two to hobble over to Mandalgarh, which being in the North East meant a step closer to the convalescing Sultan. And didn't the Rajputs let them have it! So much so that Ghiyas-ud-Din, now in a worse shape than ever, struck in both arms and legs declared surrender and retired, or better still was transported to his capital Mandu in the South East, from whence he never came forth again.

This allowed for the Sisodian Maharana to install himself once more in Chittor, which meant finding a place for his faithful Rajputs to live in. "I have decided," Raimal said one day as he placed one hand on Sajja's shoulder and the other on Ajja's shoulder while walking in the Darbar[35], "to reward you both for your services- you must each have a jagir... a small kingdom of your own, so to speak." Raimal turned and looked at Ajja, "I will give you Bari Sadri, so you will be below me, South East of Chittorgarh." He then turned towards Sajja, "And to you, I will give Delwara, above me, North West of Chittorgarh, and while you are there," Raimal continued to speak with Sajja, "you can keep an eye on Gogunda-Kumbha, my father," Raimal raised his eyes upwards to the heavens, "Lord

---

35   Royal courtyard

Ekling, guide his pre mature transformation," the Maharana interceded the god at the thought of Udai, his brother slaying their father Khumba. "My father knew how handy a fort would be in the middle of the Aravalli Range. Mind you," Raimal said turning quickly towards Sajja again, "so did the medieval Rajputs. Ah… I can't imagine Mewar surviving from those Sultans without the Aravalli hills to bar their way. Yes," Raimal concluded, "you must keep your eyes on Gogunda."

However, in spite of Raimal's good intentions of each living in a kingdom of their own, it was not long before they had to come together again; because even though the Maharana had installed himself at Chittorgarh, peace had not. Since the Malwa Sultan failed in subjecting the Ruler of Mewar to the Lodi Kingdom, the Lodi King of Delhi himself thought he would do better, but in spite of relentless attempts; Raimal, his five sons, together with Ajja and Sajja had always managed to come out on top- not unscathed, mind you- but always winners they were and the Lodi King could not get his hands on the Mewar Kingdom by a long run.

Although Raimal was a warrior worth his salt and the Rajputs at his service were no less worthy; the fighters who tipped the scales in Raimal's favour were nonetheless his sons and the one who stood out above the rest was Raimal's third born, Sangram- not because he had a crippled leg and had lost one of his hands in battle but because, in spite of being third born, he was destined to be king. It was this premonition that irritated the reckless first born, Prithvi, who had no intention of stepping aside and was forever setting a snare for his brother to fall into, so Sangram would accidentally, Prithvi hoped, be called to the next world.

In all fairness to Sangram, more affectionately known as Sanga, the premonition that one day he would be king was not the only reason that made him stand out above the rest of his siblings since the first and second born of Raimal's sons apart from being ferocious on the field, and not only on the field, had nothing else to recommend them. However, with such hardly peace seeking siblings it meant there was never a dull moment in the Mardana, the men's quarters and with the second born, Jaimal, there was never a dull moment in the Zenana, the women's quarters.

In order to settle the matter an astrologer was called to predict the three Princes's future in the presence of many Sardars and other nobles including Raimal's uncle Sarangdeo who was most revered by the Maharana. As soon as the astrologer, a woman, said she saw the Kingdom written on Sangram's head, Prithvi leap on his younger sibling and struck Sanga as hard as he could. Sanga retaliated and left his two brothers consumed with wounds while he himself gashing from five sword injuries and an arrow in his eye escaped near death. Their uncle admonished Prithvi for his shameful behaviour and it was not at all fitting to fight for the throne while their father was still alive. When Raimal heard of the happening and was told that Sanga had an empty eye socket he burst into anger as a disfigurement in a royal person would preclude that person from ascending the throne. But the King's anger was to no avail, the hole would not be fixed, Sangram's face was disfigured, there was no way his eye could be recuperated, the Sardars assured the Maharana.

"That's the last straw!" Raimal shouted furiously, "None of my sons will ever inherit my kingdom if this behaviour persists!" Fearing that next time, Prithvi would not limit himself to strike out the other eye, Sanga ran off with his uncle into hiding and Raimal banished his troublesome first born, Privthi, to the reclusion of Kumbhalgarh until he learned to behave himself. In the meantime, Raimail did as he threatened he would and started transferring his lands elsewhere, namely into the care of his uncle Sarangdeo, causing the blood to rise in the banished Prithvi who foresaw that he would not even inherit the tufts of grass beneath his feet, let alone a kingdom. So, with the pretext of helping his father against the Sultan forces, Prithvi found the opportunity to run his sword through his great uncle Sarangdeo's intestines and thus eliminating he who had benefited of Mewar's lands. After which he attempted to end the life of his father's brother, Surajmal, who had also been designated as carer of Mewar's lands but Prithvi failed on this occasion, however he was threatening enough to convince his uncle to abandon Mewar and set up his own kingdom elsewhere, all dutifully discussed over a refreshing cup of tea. But back in the tent, as Surajmal's wife was preparing a bowl of food for Prithvi containing an essence that would procure eternal sleep she calculated it a neat way of ending the matter- but since her husband was hungry and wanted to eat too, her plan was thwarted as she had to throw away the contents to avoid poisoning also Surajmal.

Whether or not the Maharana, Prithvi's father, was pleased or otherwise by the deeds of his Crown Prince, it is not known; the fact remains that Prithvi returned to his exile in Kumbhalgarh where he continued his relentless exploits. By this time, Prithvi had managed to gather around himself sixteen wives but nothing is known about having any sons, except one, Banbir. However, none of Prithvi's official ladies ever laid claim to having had this child but Banbir, nevertheless existed and stuck to his father so zealously that when Prithvi was out on one of his renown and illegitimate excursion and his brother-in-law served him a cup that caused Prithvi to return back, in great haste, to Kumbhalgarh where he laid down his head and lifted it no more; Banbir swore that one way or another he himself would sit on the throne of Mewar even if his father had not.

Meanwhile Jaimal, the Maharana's second born, another hot headed youth, dedicated most of his exploits to the women's quarters, until a Solanki Rajput put an end to Jaimal's temporal existence when the latter expressed the desire to put his hands on the Solanki's daughter. Raimal thinking his first three sons dead racked his brains as what to do. "This is my thirty-sixth year as Ruler of Mewar, I'm not as young as I used to be," Raimal one day lamented to his faithful Rajputs and Elders, who could do nothing but nod their heads in agreement. "And I have no heir…"

"But Sire, you have ten other sons left!" Ajja said.

"And eleven queens!" Sajja added with a gleam.

"No," Raimal said firmly, "Prithvi, Jaimal and Sanga are all dead in order to get the throne… I'll have no other son on this throne when I'm gone," Raimal said thoughtfully as he looked across to his young and perhaps not too bright cousin Jesa as a possible heir.

"But Sanga's body has never been found, he may still be alive," Ajja said.

"How I wish- he would have made a great Maharana even with only one eye…" Raimal said stung with regret, "but after Prithvi killed his great uncle where would Sanga find protection? He has probably been torn apart by the wild beasts in the forest."

"I think not, Sire," Ajja began…

"How's that?" Raimal questioned, quite puzzled, "Have you any intelligence on the matter."

"There is talk of a great warrior in the south east of Ajmer who is at the service of the Paramara chief of Srinagar…"

"And…?" Raimal demanded.

"This warrior alone has stopped his chief's lands from being annexed… A savage lion against the Delhi Sultan…"

"That must be Sanga!" Raimal whispered to himself. "Who is this chief? The name of the Chief!"

"Rao Karamchand, Sire."

"Go to him, find this chief… offer him lands, wives, elephants… anything! But bring back Sanga!"

"I thought you wanted me to sit on the Gaddi, cousin…" Jesa said, suddenly waking up.

"You'll find yourself sitting on a cactus, if you are not carefully," one of the court Elders snapped.

"My cousin Sanga cannot sit on the throne…"

"Oh," Raimal said with a threatening look, "and why is that not to be?"

"He's a crippled…" Jesa yelled childishly. "Sanga has no eye, no hand and no teeth…"

"You'll soon have no balls- if you don't keep quiet," the Maharana admonished.

"It's true… A disabled Ruler can't sit on the throne of Mewar. It's the law!" Jesa insisted.

"You'll be more than disabled if you say another word!" the Elder said grabbing Jesa by the back of his neck and hurling him out of the tent.

So it was that Sanga was brought back to the Mewar court and with him came the chief, Rao Karamchand, from whom he would not be separated and who was made a member of the Mewar Government. On May 24th of Raimal's 36th year reign, at the death of his father, Sanga sat on the Gaddi and became, disabled or not, Mewar's Fiftieth Ruler. As Ajja and Sajja served Raimal, now swore to serve his son just as faithfully; and since the name Sangram means 'War', for the following eighteen years of this Ruler's reign, no prizes are given as to guess what took place. Yet, this war hound was capable of great acts of peace as his father Raimal was in liberating Sultan Muzaffar, for a reasonable sum of money of course. Sanga overrode the financial part when Muzaffar's successor, Bahadur, asked for Sanga's help in outwitting his brothers in obtaining the throne of Gujarat. Sanga considered having a friend on the throne of Gujarat an asset so he Bahadur was given asylum and assistance at the court of Chittor. Little did Sanga know that history was about to repeat itself referring to when Ratan courteously escorted Ala-ud-din to the gate, that in the years to come the house of Mewar would have to pay an equally bitter price for Sangram's kindness to the ungrateful guest.

CHAPTER NINE

Mira Bai at the Court of Sangram and Victory on the Battle field- 1526

Death of Crown Prince Bhojraj; his uncouth brother Ratan becomes Crown Prince; Sangram wins back lands lost to the Muslim forces

The lack of a hand, a leg and an eye did not prevent Sanga from having more than twice as many wives as his father, twenty-eight in all, maybe it was all due to his large eyes- or at least the one he had left, and immense muscular strength. However he had only seven (known) sons, three of which are sucked into oblivion as in one way or another did not manage to outlive their father: and strangely enough, apart from he who should have reigned, Crown Prince Bhojraj: the other three, in turn, became Rulers of Mewar.

Crown Prince Bhojraj gained quite a reputation for having married Mira Bai, a mystic poetess. The two Jhala brothers, on the rare occasions when they were at the Mewar court in Chittor and not at their Jagirs or on the battlefield with Sanga, were able to admire the charm and talented verses of this Rajput Princess, great-granddaughter of the founder of Jodhpur, orphaned at a tender age and worshipper of god Krishna. Once, Sajja had the occasion to ask her what was the little statue of a goat herd that she kept carrying around with her. She told him this was no goat heard but it was a statue of god Krishna as Girdhar Gopal, in other words, a cowherd. "It was given to me by a sadhu (a holy man) who was visiting Merta just after my mother died. Since then I have always worshipped Krishna as my Divine Lover," Mira Bai concluded. Sajja looked at her pensively.

"But now you have another lover…" Mira Bai looked astonished. "A human lover…" Sajja quickly corrected himself realizing he was treading on sacrilegious grounds by comparing Kunwar Bhojraj to the Deity of Lord Krishna. The fact that Bhojraj was Crown Prince and heir to the now most powerful and prestigious throne of Mewar did not mean that Sajja could place him on the same footing as Lord Krishna. "Would it not be best if you put the statue in a temple...?"

"Oh no!" Mira Bai interrupted quickly, "I cannot separate myself from this image," she stopped and thought, "But yes, I must have a temple for Lord Krishna and myself alone."

"Have you not got one?" Sajja asked surprised.

"No, all the temples here are for everyone- I do not have one just for myself," she paused, "but I have not been here long enough to have one built."

"Then you must ask Maharana Sangram to build you one."

"Yes, of course, I must... where is my Father-in-Law?" Naturally Sangram was under his tent planning the next battle campaign with Ajja, other Sardars, and the coloured pillows, as his father would have done. On either side of the orange pillow which denoted Chittor were two other pillows. The purple one, Malwa was to the South East of the orange pillow and the green one, Gujarat was South West of the orange pillow. "These two Sultans," Sanga said as he thrust a lance into the purple and the green pillows on either side of the orange one are under our control."

'I should say so Sire," Ajja said, "the Sultan of Malwa is a guest in our prison..."

"Indeed," Sanga answered pulling out the lance from the purple pillow, "I thought it was best to take precautions- these Sultans from Mandu have always been the worst, until they learn their lesson like that predecessor Ghiyas-ud-Din."

"Mandalgarh! What a battle that was!" Ajja cried, recalling how the now defunct Sultan Ghiyas-ud-Din was defeated.

"I think this Sultan here, Mahmud, grovelling in our prisons has learnt his lesson too," The Maharana said thoughtfully.

"You're not thinking of releasing him?" Ajja promted.

"At a price! Besides, a Sultan without territory is quite harmless." Sanga turned as Sajja entered with Mira Bai. "Ah, my enchanting daughter-in-law..." the Maharana said not too pleased by her presence. "What may you be doing wandering away from your quarters?"

"Looking for a temple."

"A temple? There are numberless temples in the palace."

"She means her own temple," Sajja explained.

"Yes Father," Bhojraj intervened. "Streams of people come to beg my wife's intercession because they know she is the chosen one of Lord Krishna."

"So, you see Father," Mira Bai said, "I need a temple of my own where I can put the image of Lord Krishna." The Maharana looked at her thoughtfully, "Even if it is only small, Father," she whispered as she bowed to leave.

"I think, we may well renovate the empty temple next to our Kumbh Shyam Temple," the Maharana said to his son Bhojraj, "Our Grandfather Kumbha built Kumbh Shyam Temple for his wife, his favourite, may I say- and as fate would have she too was called Mira Bai." Sanga paused and looked at the Crown Prince thoughtfully, "if your wife is as popular as people say she is, the Kumbh Shyam will come in handy if there is an over spill of pilgrims," he then smoothed his pointed moustache, "looks as if I'll have to be careful with that one," the Maharana said undertone to Sajja, "she's still in her teens, but she could become quite a handful, later."

"How could my brother marry such a woman?" Ratan, the Maharana's third son complained sulkily.

"Are you questioning my decision on the marriage of the Crown Prince?" Rana Sanga asked threateningly. Ratan slouched back in his corner without a word.

"Oh, come on brother," Karen, the Maharana's second son, interrupted himself as he coughed- his lungs were not his best assets, "I find her love songs enlightening."

"It's discussing to have one's bride dedicate love songs to another..." Ratan growled, "even if that other is a god."

"Now brother, you mustn't blaspheme... Bhojraj is fortunate to have a bride to intercede on his behalf to a god," Karen scolded still coughing. Ratan rubbed his foot in the ground.

"Mewar can do better for an heir than have such a flimsy minded Crown Prince! Ratan whined.

"Who? You, for instance brother? Don't forget you're third in line, after me..."

"you're not going to last out the year are you?" Ratan said cruelly.

"There's always cousin Banbir..." Karen said not at all discouraged.

"That Bastard!"

"Even so," Karen began, "as he is the only surviving son of our uncle Prithvi who was Crown Prince whereas our father was only third in line, Banbir claims he is the rightful heir to the throne of Mewar."

"Over my dead body! His father may have been Crown Prince, but a dead one when our father took the throne."

"What's this?" Rana Sanga interrupted angrily, "My sons fighting over the throne?"

"You and your brothers, were no better. Father, you were no example to follow, now were you?" Ratan said glibly.

"And you will find yourself in exile if you do not moderate your speech." The Maharana said abruptly. "Bhojraj is the heir to the throne, not simply because he is first born," Sangram continued with severity, "but because he has proven to be worthy as I proved to be so in exile when fighting for my Lord and protector Karamchand... I took up the chattra, the royal standard..."

"That was not courage that was foolishness!" Ratan sneered, "Getting killed in place of Karamchand who was not your father, and it was not your throne, nor your land..."

"But the gods preserved me, I did not get killed but survived to sit on my father's throne because those two bastards of my brothers before me managed to get themselves ingloriously killed: the first Prithvi, whom Banbir thinks was his father and claims this throne from me but has not got the guts to face me, was poisoned by his own brother-in-law; and the second born, Jaimal, ended up just as foolishly, struck by the sword of the father of one of the damsals he was messing about with in Gujarat. And you..." Rana Sanga pointed directly at Ratan, "You are going to end up the same way!" Maharana Sanga walked back to his pillows again, "I certainly would never let you ride in battle as my chief," he said turning towards Ratan, "I don't think you know what a chattra is, let alone take it up and perhaps die in place of your Lord!" The Maharana concentrated on the pillows and made an addition. There was a bold black pillow above the orange Chittor. "That," the Maharana said to Ajja as he pointed to the black pillow, "is Delhi and that sow Ibrahim who is their Lodi Emperor has to go!" The Maharana turned on his good leg, "Ibrahim got rid of his predecessor which did us a favour as Sikander had nothing better to do than eat away at our lands... But..." the Maharana stamped, "that sow has dared to do the same thing!" The trusted Rao Karamchand walked slowly towards the Maharana.

"Sire," he said thoughtfully, "Our lands now stretch to Gujarat, Malwa and Bayana, none of these were ours before... All the Princes of Marwar and Jaipur pay you homage; the Raos of Gwalior, Sikri, Kalpi, Raisen, Chanderi, Ajmer, Bundi Abu, Gagron and Rampura are your tributaries..."

he paused, "we have already won fifteen battles against the Muslims- there comes a time when we should seek peace..." The Maharana put his good arm around Rao Karamchand's shoulders and said,

"I love you even more than I loved my own father, faithful Karamchand, and never will I forget it was you who took me into your home when I was in exile and everyone believed I was a goat heard- but I am a warrior, not a king- a trustee of Mewar and so I must protect its territories." Rao Karamchand bowed his head and said no more. "My Crown Prince Bhojraj and I will head five Raos, one seventy eight Rawals and their Rawats, four and half thousand horsemen and three hundred war elephants.

Months later Sangram returned victorious, he had defeated the Sultan Ibrahim Lodi of Dehli but he had lost his son Bhojraj. The price was too high for Sangram and he returned with head bowed low as if he had been defeated; there were no cries of victory or effusions of joy. Meantime, during the Maharana's absence, his second son, Karen, died of pneumonia and much to Ratan's delight; he was now the heir to the throne of Mewar! All along the journey home, as they carried the wounded body of Bhojraj, Ajja had hoped the Crown Prince would recover as Ajja couldn't envisage staking his life in battle for an uncouth being such as Ratan. Alongside Ajja, his brother Sajja and all the other nobles shared the same hope; but as they saw the hill of Chittorgarh, only Sangram knew that his Crown Prince would not see another dawn. In effect, as soon as Bhojraj touched the ground of his palace, he drew his long but final sigh.

Mira Bai ran and threw herself distraught on her husband's corpse. "I thought I heard someone say time back," Ratan smirked to his father, "that my brother was fortunate to have a wife to intercede to the gods on his behalf."

"And so it is!" Sangram retaliated, "Your brother is eternal- death cannot touch him now," he paused menacingly, "which is something I cannot say for you."

"His wife will also be eternal within the next twenty four hours..." Ratan said complacently. Sangram, with the one good eye he had, thrust him a piercing look of condemnation. "As the law commands Father," Ratan paused as if helplessly, "Mira Bai must be placed on the funeral pyre with her husband!"

"No! Never!" Mira Bai looked upwards, firmly, at her father-in-law, "My only husband is Lord Krishna, I cannot die... I must live and dedicate my life to god Vishnu and having married into the house of Mewar I am to pay homage to god Ekling, the god of Mewar."

"She has too many gods to tend for, as far as I'm concerned," Ratan sneered.

"You pagan!" Sangram retorted, "Krishna is but a manifestation of the god Vishnu!" Sangram took Mira Bai's hand, "You are right," he whispered. Then turning indignantly to his son said, "Being a Mewar bride she is to pay homage to god Ekling or have you forgotten that god Ekling is the true ruler of Mewar and the Maharana is but his trustee?" Ratan turned towards the Sardars;

"When I sit on that throne," he boasted, "you will all do as I say, not what the gods of my sister-in-law says- is that understood?"

"I for one hope, never to see that day," Ajja said proudly.

"You may indeed not be here to see it!" Ratan scoffed.

"Enough!" Sangram bellowed. "I am the unfortunate one to have to leave a kingdom such as this in the paltry hands of this my third son."

"Indeed, father, the gods have not been kind to you!" Ratan gibed.

"I can soon remedy that!" Sangram threatened.

"Who with- Vikram?" Ratan sneered to himself, "he's hardly old enough to stand on his feet." Sangram looked downwards impatiently.

"He may die in battle yet," Sangram lisped ironically to Ajja while furtively eyeing Ratan.

"And you may soon have other sons," Ajja answered.

"True!" Sangram stated, "the first ten of my wives are past it, I should think, but the other eighteen are not... especially the last one!"

The Maharana ordered the body of his Crown Prince to be prepared for the funeral and Mira Bai to be taken to her newly renovated chapel. "I won't allow it!" Ratan intercepted immediately.

"What won't you allow, you miserable, contemptible peanut!" Sangram bellowed.

"Mira Bai must be placed on the funeral pyre with her husband!"

"Haven't you heard who her husband is now?" Sangram retorted. "So, unless you can bring me the dead reincarnated corpse of the god Krishna, I cannot satisfy your demand."

"It's the law!" Ratan howled. "You can't bring shame on the house of Mewar by placing your Crown Prince without a woman on the funeral pyre!"

"Who said Bhojraj will burn alone?" Sangram paused. "There are plenty of concubines in the Palace Zenana- just choose one or two... or any amount of number that will satisfy your refined sense of justice," Sangram waved his hand impatiently as if to send Ratan away.

"That Mira Bai will not have an easy life when I'm Maharana," Ratan sneered behind Sangram's back.

"I'm not dead yet!" Sagram said vehemently as he turned suddenly.

The following year in 1522, on the 4ᵗʰ August, Sangram's fifth son, Udai, was born from Sangram's favourite wife Karmavati of Bundi; followed by Parbat and finally Krishna named so to spite Ratan, who however, did not see his fifth year. Whether it was the euphoria of having given birth to another three sons or not which spurned Sangram to march into battle once more and conquer the north, it is not easy to say, but Sangram was determined that Delhi would be his. Although Ibrahim, the Lodi leader had attempted now and again to challenge the Mewar Ruler, once more, Sangram had never had much difficulty in suppressing the aggression; although many of Sangram's Chieftains would have preferred if their leader would turn a blind eye, (the only one he had left), to the Sultan's provocation as they, had not the passion for war running through their blood that Sangram had, and frankly were sick and tired and fed up of war! But the Mewar Chieftains need not have worried for someone else, coming from afar; as far as Afghan in the North West invaded Dehli and not only defeated Ibrahim but took his head off too. Then, this invader, the name being Babur, getting rid of the Lodi dynasty, established his own and thus the Mughal Empire was well and truly formed. The year was 1526.

CHAPTER TEN

Barbur and the beginning of the Mughal Empire to the 2nd Sack of Chittor 1534

Agra replaces Delhi as the Mughal capital; Rajputs defaulting to the Mughals at the battle of Khanwa; the death of Sanga; Ratan begins his persecution of Mira Bai; after his death; Ratan is replaced by his other ill-mannered brother, Vickram

The complete suppression of Ibrahim was something that the gallant Rajput Maharana had never seriously considered to undertake, but since it had happened it might have been met with gratefulness were it not for the fact that someone even more ferocious had taken the Sultan's place. This factor spurred the already heated Sangram to boiling point and he mustered together the whole of his Royal power adding even more elements to his inflated train of one hundred and four Rawats, eight thousand horsemen and five hundred war elephants. This Mughal Emperor, Barbur, simply could not install himself on the throne, even if not at Delhi itself but at Agra and oversee the whole of Northern India- that place- Sangram argued, was reserved for himself, the Mewar Ruler.

"The Mewar throne has existed for nearly a thousand years and now we have an Emperor in Agra! We must drive that Babur out of the whole of India," the Maharana said taking his faithful Ajja to one side, "drive him back to where he came from, Afghanistan. I will have no foreign Emperor on an Indian throne or their strange religions where women can marry who they like, even when their husbands are dead! Can you imagine that Ajja?" the Maharana said emphatically. "Widows marrying another man! Beyond belief! And there's no such thing to these Muslim as Sati. None of their women are placed on a funeral pyre alongside their dead husbands where they belong..." Sangram shook his head forcefully, "No, this Babur must go!"

"My Lord," Rao Karamchand, began as he neared the Maharana, "Our Rawals are weary of all these wars! The Emperor will not challenge your power as your fame of being unconquerable is renown- you are able to count not one, or two, not even five or ten even, but well eighteen victories against the Muslims!" Sangram limped towards Karamchand.

"My most honoured and much loved protector, I cannot deny you anything," Sangram paused, "I promise you once I have vanquished that usurper, there'll be no more wars... this will be our last battle!" Sangram then walked up to Ajja, slapped his back hard and said, "Come Ajja, let's prepare... war awaits!"

At the beginning of the year 1527, the Maharana of Mewar, the great Rana Sanga, led an impressive army consisting of the seven main Rulers of the Rajput confederacy, nine Raos and one hundred and four Rawats who commanded over eighty thousand foot soldiers, one hundred thousand horsemen and five hundred war elephants. They marched towards Agra, about five hundred km North East, where Babur had installed his throne. The two armies met at Khanwa, sixty km West of Agra where Rana Sanga completely destroyed the fifteen hundred strong advance Imperial Guard. As always, however, when an alliance of Rajput Leaders come together in war there is never a straight forward agreement on anything and the more Babur's warriors strengthened themselves in the trenches the more dissipated the Mewar forces became. Nevertheless Rana Sanga led a ferocious attack aimed towards the middle and to the right side of the Imperial forces; the intense and bloody slaughter lasted many hours. Babur soon put into action his usual military tactics that so far had always made him victorious. At the centre where Sanga hurled his attack Babur had placed a barrier of wagons allowing passage ways for the artillery and cavalry assaults whilst on the side he had wheeling cavalry charging. Babur's artillery destroyed the Rajputs forces which were placed in rows side by side, his cannons fired unto the elephants and his cavalry charges from the sides, tactics quite unseen in Mewar completely disoriented the Rajputs. But what really tore in the Maharan's soul was that Silahadi, Sangram's most trusted General, perhaps despairing of ever winning, defaulted to the Mughal side.

Maharana Sanga had more wounds on his flesh than feathers on a bird, but still he refused to surrender until a powerful arrow whizzed across the sky and hit him full in the eye which knocked him unconscious. Ajja, aghast immediately donned the Maharana's tunic. "Babur must not know the Maharana has fallen!" He cried to the troops. "We will continue the battle!" Ajja ordered as he took up the Chattra, the Royal Standard with the golden sun, the symbol of the Maharana. From a distance Ratan saw Ajja's courageous deed- "The fool!" Ratan murmured with envy, "He's asking to be killed!" But in spite of the knowledge that by displaying himself the royal umbrella he would be the prime target, Ajja continued to fight with intense courage until a blade from the enemy struck deep into his breast, from which it was mercifully removed by his brother Sajja who decreed that the Mewar Royal insignia should remain with the descendants of his brother Ajja at Bari Sadri who have ever since considered it a great privilege to represent their Lord when ever it is necessary.

After the battle the Maharana was taken to the fort of Ranthambor where supposedly recovered. Thus, Rana Sanga did not die on the battlefield as one may rightfully suppose; that honour was reserved to Ajja from Halvad. Neither did the Mighty Sanga die at Chittor, to where he had vowed he would not return unless in victory- indeed the Maharana was planning another attack to take place shortly: but be it the countless wounds or a potion offered to him by his faithful Sardars who were not too inclined to engage in another battle yet; the fact remains that Maharana Sangram Singh died on Mewar's northern border at Baswa without seeing the glory of victory ever again.

On the day of his enthronement which was the following February in 1528, Ratan Singh breathed a much relieved "At last!" He allowed himself lavish celebration and free reign to his macabre jubilation of being rid, not only of his father, the Ruler, but also of Ajja, who dying on the battlefield in place of the Maharana could no longer coerce Ratan's insidious desire for power. As for Sajja, Ratan could easily confine him to Delwara, the estate Maharana Raimal endowed on him. Then he ordered that his widowed sister-in-law, Mira Bai stop her nonsense. Ratan told his chief wife, "I'm not having the court of Mewar overrun by beggars and get that woman to stop wearing saffron. Saffron is the colour of Rajputs engaged in war- she is only making a mockery of tradition…"

And for the rest of his four year reign Ratan spent it in accumulating as many enemies as he could. One of these was the Hara Prince Surajmal of Bundi who in a failed attempt to get him crushed by one of the Palace elephants and passing it off as an unfortunate accident, Ratan decided to try again but Surajmal, now being on his guard struck back and managed to literally slice Ratan in two, from the throat to the navel. Nevertheless,

Surajamal too died from the blows received during the combat. Thus, in 1531 Ratan's fourteen year old brother Vikramaditya II became the ruler of Mewar.

Ratan may have had his faults but he was capable of retaining his leadership to the end. Retaining one's leadership as a Mewar Ruler, any Ruler for that matter, is by no means an easy task, since one only has the power that others are willing to concede. The nobles and chiefs that surrounds a Ruler are as powerful, if not more powerful than the Ruler himself. History is dotted with examples of such, and perhaps one of the most impressive is that of the successor to the Great Kumbha. The real successor to Maharana Kumbha was his Crown Prince Raimal, but Udai, one of Kumbha's younger sons decided that since his older brother was in exile, it was time to get rid of the father and usurp the throne. Thus after murdering Kumbha, Udai had to bribe others from outside the kingdom in order to stay in power which was only a mere five years as he was soon to be struck by lightning or something of such providential manner and his name had been wiped out from all records. Another example in the reverse is Sangram himself, who not only had never been Crown Prince as he was third in line but also with a few limbs missing was proclaimed Maharana in spite of a tradition that forbade a disabled ruler to be enthroned. But the nobles wanted him because he was able to scare the pants off anyone who got in the way of Mewar- and his Sarders made sure they got what they wanted.

However, things can become tricky when the one next in line and hence rightful heir of which there is no dispute, is someone that simply cannot be digested by anyone at court. This happened to Vikramaditya when the Sarders discovered that the fourteen year old heir was nothing but an insolent, vindictive brat. Nevertheless in 1531, in want of anything better, Vikramaditya was declared the fifty-second ruler of Mewar and the consequences of such ill matched enthronement soon became evident. For one thing the crystal beauty of Mira Bai's notes of the songs with which she worshipped her Lord started to get on his nerves. "I'm not having that woman shrill down my ear drums morning noon and night," he protested to some priests who were seeking substantial favours from the Maharana. "And now she has taken to defile the house of Mewar by dishonouring her husband's name."

"Really, how?" One of the priests asked.

"She has a man- a cobbler- Ravidas." The priests gazed on in some amazement. "I've put my spies onto her," Vikramaditya persuaded. "She gets dressed up as a servant and they meet in the village- and now she sings songs about him, here in my Temple!"

"A terrible affair…" the priests shook their heads, "A Rajput Princess with one of so low-caste- it's inadmissible!"

"Ravidas?" One of the more simpleton priests asked, "Ravidas the Saint?"

"Be quiet you fool!" the other priest murmured as he motioned the simpleton to silence.

"Did someone speak?" The arrogant Maharana demanded.

"My Lord," the chief priest began, "I humbly suggest you engage that delightful girl cousin of yours, Udabai to persuade your sister-in-law to change her ways."

"Ah! My late brother Bhojraj cousin! Ravishing girl!" The young Maharana sucked his lips sensually at the thought. "Splendid! And what else!"

"Public abuse, which I will stir up myself!" The chief priest volunteered.

Some time later, in spite of the public abuse where Mira Bai ran home in shame to hide in her temple and Udabai's efforts of persuasion ended in becoming a convert and devotee of Lord Krishna herself, Vikramaditya decided to pass to stronger measures. He arranged for one of his concubines to take a poisoned cup of cordial, yet although Mira Bai drank it fully, nothing happened, not the slightest ache or vomit, miraculously Mira Bai was spared of the evil consequence. Vikramaditya put it down to some herbs she had taken beforehand to safeguard herself from such things happening. So, he then employed a snake charmer from among his mercenary paiks and wrestlers with which he had surrounded himself in preference to the Rajput warriors, to place a poisoned viper inside a basket of fresh blooms offering it in homage to Mira Bai. Yet when she opened the basket, among the flowers she only saw a small image of Krishna. Finally, her uncle in Merta, being told of his niece's dilemma summoned her back home. This was rather providential because the Sultan of Gujarat, Bahadur Shar, who was waiting in the wings to avenge his predecessor Muazaffar who when he had been taken prisoner and ransomed by Raimal swore to settle the score one day hence decided to take advantage of the discord at the Mewar court and attack Chittor.

"That's his excuse, Muazaffar," Sajja declared as the Mewar Rajputs met to plan their campaign. "Is it not rather the silver that has just been excavated in our Zawar Mines which Badhur finds more attractive?" Sajja paused with a look of bitterness. "Gujarat- my homeland- and Mewar were once brethren but since it has fallen into Muslim hands only greed surmounts."

"And to think father," the young Jait said, "the great Maharana Sanga offered this scoundrel protection under the palace roof."

"And how did he repay the good Sanga then?" Sajja shook his head, "by fooling around in the Zenana and tampering with our women... A Rajput Princess is to prefer death to dishonouring her people by conceding herself to a Muslim!"

"Good Sajja," Rawat Bagh Singh of Deolia began, "Bahadur's forces are advancing and we must protect Mewar's line of succession. I propose we send Maharana Vikramaditya," the Rawat paused, "with his mercenary paiks of course, since he has no preference for Rajputs... I suggest he goes north to Bundi which can be used as a staging ground."

"And Prince Udai?" Sajja asked.

"We can send him with his nurse Panna Dhai and his Mother the Queen to safety in Bundi, the homeland of Rajmata Karmavati," Rao Karamchand proposed.

"But that leaves Chittor without a Maharana and only royalty can defend the capital," the heir of Bundi who had brought five hundred Haras with him, objected.

"We can crown Rawat Bagh as the temporary representative of the Maharana," Sajja proposed. Upon which all the Chiefs and Rawats concurred.

"Let's go through our positions," Rawat Bagh stated after his temporary coronation. "My troops and I will take charge of the second gateway, Bhairon Pol; Solanki Bhairondas of Desuri will take charge of the third gate, Hanuman Pol; and Jhala Sajja will be on Ganesh Pol, the fourth gateway.

Bahadur employed Portuguese artillery and engineers. They dug a tunnel under the western side of the hill of Chittor and continued to dig as far as the foundations of the fortress then stacked explosives next to the main rampart where the Hara troops were posted. The explosion destroyed much of the main wall killing most of the Hara troops. The other Rawats, Durga, Sonigira of Jalore and the Raos of Mount Abu came to their aid and fought viciously against the continuing attacks.

In the meantime, troops from Mandu of Malwa attacked Vikramaditya in the north and although the Maharana fought back fiercely, his mercenary paiks were no Rajputs and seeing that no good would come by staying in the north, those few Rajput warriors that had accompanied the Maharana returned to Chittor to defend their capital. As war raged in Chittor it was the turn of the Ganesh Pol, the fourth gateway where Sajja was stationed with his troops. The immense blast that followed wiped out those that had come to the replace the already dead. Jait, from some distance saw the destruction of his father Sajja and the thirty two thousand Rajput troops stationed in defence.

Seeing that Chittor had fallen, Rajmata Karmavati gathered all the women of Chittorgarth and prepared a funeral pyre. She would lead them in the Jauhar before the enemy Bahadur Shar would enter the fort and take possession. Led by the Queen Mother, being and having remained, Maharana Sangram's favourite wife, about thirteen thousand Rajput women sacrificed themselves on the flames in this second sack of Chittor. The year being 1534. However, this immense sacrifice could have been spared as far as Bahadur Shah was concerned, because he indeed never had the chance to take possession of Chittor; the great Mughal Emperor Humayun, (Barbur's successor) had invaded Gujarat forcing Bahadur to abandon his exploits at Chittor, while Humayun himself had a half hearted go at capturing Chittor, which as fate would have it, he did not, probably because he was not so much concerned in capturing Chittor as to prevent Bahadur from getting his hands on it as a foolish teenager was much easier to keep under control than a weathered Sultan.

Thus Vikramaditya returned to his throne in Chittor, not without causing exasperation on all sides.

CHAPTER ELEVEN

From 1534 Udai's Exile and Reinstatement 1540

Vikramaditya placed under house arrest; Banbir elected as Regent of Mewar; Udai escapes to Kumbhalgarh; Jait of Delwara makes marriage arrangements with Marwar Rajput and disputes; a bride is also found for Udai of Mewar; Udai is proclaimed Maharana and another bride; Udai's hunting adventures with Jait's heir Man Singh(Delwara)

What were they to do they asked themselves. Everyone turned to the eldest amongst them, Karamchand of Ajmer who had shielded Sangram when in exile and from whom Sangram would not have been parted. "What about his brother, Udai?" Kanji the Choondawat Rajput leader volunteered.

"I'm still in my teens myself," Jait Singh, the son of the much mourned Sajja, lamented, "But Udai is not even a teenager yet! We don't want to get the reputation of having a kindergarten instead of a throne, now do we?" He paused, then struck his breast forcibly, "My father Sajja gave his life for that empty pumpkin Vikramaditya, and I am not going to stay here to suffer the same fate.

"Son, where are you to go?" Karamchand, asked concerned. "You are a Rajput of the Jhala house of Gujarat, your father has been with us since the great Maharana Raimal..." Jait listened quietly and shook his head, "What of Delwara... Maharana Raimal's gift to your father, are you to leave that?"

"I refuse to serve infants on a throne! I will go north to Marwar, Jodhpur. Rao Maldeo has offered me the kingdom of Kherwa in exchange..." Jait looked around at the elders, "My father has gone, there is nothing left for me here."

"Will you not stay?" Karamchand beckoned.

"There is no pride for a Rajput to serve an empty throne… and until there is a proper Lord, for me the throne of Mewar is empty."

"Jait's right," Banbir agreed, who in the meantime, after the death of his uncle Sangram, had managed to place himself at the services of his cousin's court, with half an eye on the throne for himself, of course. "There are t-w-o many infants as heirs… Besides, Udai may turn out as insolent as his brother."

"That remains to be seen," Karamchand said wisely, "Although by the sparkle in his eye, I suspect Udai to have a nobler disposition."

The Elder was not aware that as he was speaking Vikramaditya was eavesdropping behind one of the walls of the darbar where the full court was assembled. Vikramaditya leaped out from his hiding place and struck the Elder across the face so forcibly that Karamchand fell to the ground. "Traitors! All of you!" Vikramaditya yelled as he stormed out of the darbar while the entire assembly of nobles rose indignantly at the affront that their revered Elder was made subject to.

"Herewith, brother Chiefs, we have had but a smell of the blossom; now we shall be obliged to eat the fruit," Kanji said bitterly.

"Tomorrow, its flavour will be known," Karamchand added.

"Unless we prune it," Kanji was provident to say. "I propose firstly, to remove Vikramaditya from the responsibility and privilege of Ruler of Mewar…" an uproar in favour of the proposal arouse from the assembly. "And secondly, to place the said person under palace arrest!" Again another uproar of agreement came forth spontaneously.

"And in the meantime are we to leave the throne empty?" Banbir asked slyly.

"That must be so…" Karamchand said pensively. "Until such day Udai becomes of age to be enthroned we must appoint a Regent…"

"Yourself?" Banbir proposed crafttily.

"Indeed, my days are counted," the Elder said, then slowly added but someone much younger… and who is no stranger to the throne…"

"Cousin Banbir!" exclaimed the Choondawat leader whose ancestor Choonda in the days of Lakha knew something on the matter of being deprived of primogeniture status, as Banbir claimed.

Banbir's eyes flashed furtively scrutinizing all eyes upon him. This was his moment, the moment he had waited for, ever since his father Crown Prince Prithvi had been poisoned and uncle Sangram was placed on the Ghaddi instead. Being Regent was not exactly being the Maharana, but that, Banbir promised himself, would come later after the little business of getting rid his two cousins first- Vikramditya would be no problem, no obstacle would bar his way- little Udai's case may present a little more difficult. "I'm not so sure Banbir is quite the right choice, Kanji murmured to himself as the Sardars, much to Banbir's exultation, proclaimed him Regent.

Being confined to Palace arrest did not prevent Vikramaditya from enjoying those pleasures that a life of irresponsible debauchery could offer and it was during one of those occasions when the disgraced Maharana was frolicking in the Zenana among his concubines that Banbir seized his chance to put a sword through Vikramaditya's body several times. "At least he died happy!" Banbir sneered as he pulled out the sword for the last time while the concubines fled screaming. However, Banbir was not satisfied, as he had claimed, there were t-w-o heirs too many to the throne of Mewar and immediately set himself to search out young Udai.

One of the Nautch girls (dancing girls) dashed into the rawala where Panna Dhai, the nurse maid had just put her own son and Prince Udai to bed. When he was an infant she had breast fed him having had a child herself when Udai was born. Breathless and in terror the Nautch girl told Panna Dhai what had happened in the Zenana. Immediately Panna Dhai ordered the girl to bring to her the strong manservant to take a basket down to the river. In the basket she placed the young Prince and told Udai it was a game of hide and seek and under no account was anyone to find out he was inside the basket. Broken hearted she instructed her own son to go into the Prince's bed and covered him with the royal blanket. When Banbir burst into the room he thrust his sword immediately into the body that lay in the royal bed while the nursemaid looked on in horror as Banbir murdered her son.

Anguished, Panna Dhai packed some clothes, then attended the quick cremation of her son and with tears still stinging her eyes she ran down to the river where the servant was waiting with the basket. Her aim was to reach Kumbhalgarh through the perilous rocks of the mountainous Arvallis, North West of Chittor. However, when they came to a town, the voice had spread that an unruly servant and her son had stolen from the house of Mewar and was not to be given aid, penalty the wrath of Maharana Vikramaditya. So all doors were shut upon Panna Dhai and her royal charge. Only the Bhils, always faithful to the Mewar Crown offered shelter and food as she struggled with the young Prince on the rugged paths that made their feet bleed, through the infamous Aravalli Range, past Gogunda and still further onwards through rough mountainous wilderness that even soldiers found it hard to overcome.

Once at Kumbhalgarh, the immensity overcame the solitary exiles: the width of the wall could easily accommodate six carriages and horses, the wall itself was second to none in dimension but to the Great Wall of China. Asha Depura Shah, a Jain merchant who was the governor of that area, when discovering the real identity of the young Prince offered his protection and spread the misleading news that Udai was Asha's own nephew.

In the meantime, Jait, the son of the much loved Sajja who died at the Ganesh Pol during the 2nd Sack of Chittor, had settled in Marwar where he had taken his wife, two daughters and the quiet, dutiful heir, Man Singh. The alliance between Jait and the Ruler of the Marwar Rathore Rajputs, Rao Maldeo was sealed by the latter bequeathing Jait with the Jagir of Kherwa. In return Jait gave his eldest daughter, Swarup Devi, in marriage, but she was still too young for marriage.

"You have my promise, when the time comes I will give her to you," Jait said to the impatient Maldeo while striding in the Ruler's darbar waiting for the other chiefs of Marwar to arrive.

"You know, I like them young!" Rao Maldeo said maliciously.

"She's only five years old!" Jait said striding away leaving the insufferable Rao to entertain the rest of the party.

"Ah, here come the Chauhans Rajputs from Jalore," the Rao said looking in the direction of the main gate and went to greet them as the party dismounted from their horses. "Akhey Raj Songara, You are welcome, honourable neighbour. How are things on the Golden Mount?"

"The Fortress holds fast, my esteemed Rao Maldeo," the Raj said as they embraced.

"And your daughters?"

"All spoken for?"

"How do you mean?" Rao Maldeo asked not hiding his disappointment.

"Is this not the question why we have assembled here today?" The Raj reminded, "My marriage!"

"Marriage indeed, but not yours! Or are you forgetting the throne of Mewar is in need of an heir and that heir is in need of a wife?"

"The marriage of Banbir!"

"That scoundrel is not an heir, he is a usurper!" The Raj paused. "The throne of Mewar has been empty long enough it is time for the real heir to return."

"But there is no other heir!" Rao Maldeo protested, "Banbir was the unofficial son of Prithvi Raj, who never made it to the throne because he died before his father- so Banbir should have had the throne instead of his uncle Sangram."

"Like you said, Banbir is not the official son and bastards do not inherit thrones," Raj Akhey paused, "That is why this question of marriage that we are here to discuss today is so important."

"First we must have a legitimate heir," Rao Maldeo objected.

"We have one..."

"An adopted one?"

"Indeed not..."

"Who then?" Maldeo said exasperated.

"No less than a son of the Great Sangram," Raj Akhey announced triumphantly.

"Impossible!" Maldeo said laughing cynically. Sangram's sons are all dead, Banbir saw to that.

"Banbir thought he had killed all of Sangram's sons, but Udai was spared."

"How is that possible?" Maldeo said incredulous, "I had word from Karamchand himself that Banbir had put the sword through Prince Udai the same night he had put the sword through Vikramaditya."

"But things did not go as they appeared."

"No?" Rao Maldeo prodded irritably, "And pray, how did things go?" he asked impatiently, "would you care to explain?"

"I had word from the governor of the town of Kumbhalgarh that an illustrious guest has been staying at the fortress for a few years now..."

"Yes, his nephew... my dear Raj you are not telling us anything new..."

"With a wet-nurse from the Mewar Royal Family?" As the Raj finished speaking, Maldeo's eyes switched back and forwards intuitively.

"Has... has anyone recognized this woman?" Maldeo asked in a whisper.

"I am going there myself after this assembly..."

"Do you know this woman...? Can you recognize this wet-nurse?"

"Panna Dhai, her name is Panna Dhai... No, not I personally, I have never met her- that is why I am not leaving alone."

"Oh?" was all Maldeo could say.

"I am taking Jait Singh with me... the son of the honourable Sajja of Delwara. Jait Singh not only knows Panna Dhai like his own mother but he knows Prince Udai like his own brother- should he have had one." Akhey Raj Songara looked in front of him and said, "Here comes Raj Jait himself!"

"When this business of recognition is over," Rao Maldeo said turning to Raj Akhey, "maybe you could spare one of your daughters for me."

"Take no heed of our honourable friend," Jait said, "I've already promised him my eldest daughter but she's still a child."

"Your Jeevant Kunwar is of child bearing age, is she not?" Maldeo asked Akhey.

"Yes, but as I said, all my daughters are spoken for, especially Jeevant Kunwar," Akhey answered irritably.

"Ah, I see," Maldeo said opening his eyes wide, "You plan to marry Jeevant Kunwar to the heir of Mewar... is that not the plan?"

That was indeed the plan and the whole assembly approved of it joyfully grateful that there was a strong probability that a son of the Great Sanga had survived, and who better would know than the Jhala Raj Jait who had spent the whole of his childhood at the court of Mewar? As Jait rode alongside Akhey Raj Songara, the excitement inside him grew. "I pray the magnificent sun to look down kindly on this offspring of Sisodia," Jait said to his companion. "And that it has not been just an illusion."

"Aye to that," Akhey said, "otherwise my plans to be the grandfather of the heir to the throne of Mewar have been but vain thoughts."

"Had you not better aim to be the father-in-law of the present heir to the throne of Mewar first before counting the chikens that have not hatched yet?" Jait said gamely. They rode on in silent expectation across the Marwar border into Mewar and then plunged south towards Kumbhalgarh.

"Do you not think it was rather a hasty decision to bring Jeevant Kunwar with you?" Jait asked. But Raj Akhey shook his head emphatically.

"No, I do not."

"What if it isn't Udai? What if Panna Dhai lied and it was her son she saved and not the Prince?"

"We shall see in a few days when we get there, won't we?"

"He was fourteen when I last saw him," Jait said pensive.

"So?" the Raj asked, "He'll be seventeen now, is that a problem for you?"

"No, no I don't think so," Jait said with a smile, "faces do not change in three years!"

"If the boy that the Governor of Kumbhalgarh is protecting is indeed the heir to the throne of Mewar then there is no time to lose- Udai must have a son immediately!" Raj Akhey looked at the column following behind. "Hence, the needful presence of my child bearing daughter."

"Let's hope he likes her!" Jait commented as he tried to get a glimpse of Jeevant Kunwar through the heavily curtained carriage windows in the train behind.

Some weeks later when the party had at last reached the immense walls of Kumbhalgarh, from the roof top, Udai saw the procession, "Uncle Asha, here they come," Udai cried. The Governor hurried to the boy's side.

"Are you ready, your Highness?" the Governor said with solicitude, "Remember, you are the rightful heir to the throne of Mewar and those people need to see that."

"You have taught me a multitude of things in these years…"

"They must see those royal qualities that are inborn and not the arrogance of your brother Vikramaditya." The Governor smiled, "But I need not worry about that, you are gentle of heart."

"Yes, my noble uncle, I try to be."

"I know that," the Governor said and then irritated added, "And stop calling me uncle… I am no uncle of yours!"

"Look, uncl… I mean Shah Asha, there's the carriage… is that…

"Jeevant Kunwar- your future bride. As soon as you have been recognized as the heir of Mewar you will be married and have a son…"

"Immediately?" Udai asked.

"Immediately!"

"And I have to do that… what you told me?" Udai glanced to his lower limbs.

"Without question!"

"What if I have a problem…?"

"Don't call me!" was the Governor's swift reply. He looked at Udai's puzzled face. "You just try and try again until you get it right." And of course Udai did get it right because he managed to father at least twenty sons and even more so daughters, but that's jumping ahead of time. The Governor placed his hand on the Prince's shoulder, "Go now," he admonished, "go to the darbar, you must meet them on your own."

As the procession of horses, carriages and elephants poured through the immense main entrance into the darbar of Kumbhalgarh, Udai approached the first horsemen who promptly dismounted. The servants took the horses and Raja Jait neared the Royal Figure, took a lasting look and bowed, then turning to the party claimed in a loud voice, "His Royal Highness Prince Udai of Mewar." Raja Akhey Songara neared, bowed and proclaimed:

"His Royal Majesty Maharana Udai Singh of Mewar!" the whole court bowed and paid the newly acknowledge king homage.

Within weeks all the main Rajput clans and chiefs came to pay homage to the new king: the Paramaras of Bijolia, the Saidas of Salumbar with other chiefs of the Choondwawat clan, the Chauhans of Kotharia and Bedla, Lukaran Jetawat, Jagga of Kelwa, Sanga of Bagore and Prithiraj of Sanchor. Then Udai and his father-in-law Raj Akhey Songara and much of the Marwar army marched on Chittor and ousted Banbir who had also rounded up an Army. Meanwhile, back at Kumbhalgarh, Udai's Crown Prince, Pratap, was born on May 9th 1540. That same year at Chittorgarh, the eighteen year old Maharana was crowned Fifty-third Ruler of Mewar.

Raja Jait Singh, pleased at having restored to Mewar its rightful heir returned to the Jagir of Kherwa in Marwar where Rao Maldeo was anxiously waiting to consummate his marriage with Jait's elder daughter. However after the wedding, Rao Maldeo, becoming Jait's son-in-law had access to the ladies quarters at Kherwa and on one occasion he was able to see his wife's younger sister, Kushal Kunwari, from whom Maldeo was unable to take his eyes off. Thus the love sick Maldeo rushes to Jait's quarters and not asks, but demands the hand of Jait's second daughter too in marriage, to which Jait replies that one daughter was enough for the favour of having been given Kherwa and that he had other plans for his second daughter. "And who are you scheming of making an alliance with?" The furious Maldeo demanded.

"None of your business!" Jait answered.

"A Muslim?" Maldeo's eyes widened with rage, "That's it! With a Muslim, so you can gang up on me!"

"Don't be ridiculous, my daughters are Jhala princesses and no foreign blood will blend with theirs..." Jait paused, "I bet you would have no scruples in giving my daughter's offspring to a Nawab!"

"I see nothing wrong in giving a daughter to a Nawab if she brings me half the Sultan's kingdom..."

"Traitor!" Jait said spitting vehemently on the floor. "Giving you Swarup Devi was my biggest mistake... My eldest daughter is worth a thousand Kherwas!"

"You can always give me back Kherwa…"

"Why? Can I have my daughter back in one piece? No, of course I can't" Jait remonstrated bitterly.

"Put an end to this nonsense," Maldeo said angrily, "Akheyraj is already allied to that pimp on the throne of Mewar and now you… I bet you have plans in marrying off Kushal Kunwari to the Mewar throne!"

"And if that was the case?"

"Who is going to make an alliance with me if half of Marwar supports the throne of Mewar?"

"That's your problem… you can always find consolation in the Shah at Agra… whoever that may be at this point in time as they seem to be having a competition as to who is better at killing the other."

"Don't try to change the subject; you will give me your second daughter…!

"Over my dead body will you have Kushal Kunwari!"

"That may well be!" Rao Maldeo threatened, drawing his sword. After a few near escapes, Jait at last managed to stick the point of his sword under his adversary's chin and said, "What stops me from thrusting this down your throat is that I don't want my eldest daughter to burn on your funeral pyre!" Jait swung on his heels, marched out and immediately set off to his old Jagir, Delwara, in the Kingdom of Mewar and left the dust of Marwar behind him forever.

Rao Maldeo's intuition was not mistaken. As the years passed, Jait's younger daughter, Kushal Kunwari married Udai Singh, thus Raja Jait of Delwara became Udai's father-in-law. Jait also had a young son and heir, Man Singh who having a sister at the Mewar court was a frequent visitor and became a close friend of his brother-in-law, the Maharana. However, Udai did not give his friendship to the young Man Singh so easily; first, the Maharana wanted to see if the heir of Delwara was a worthy subject for the Maharan's confidences- thus Udai put the young man to the test. Hunting was considered not only the sport of Princes but it was also an infallible way of judging the value of a man.

The wilderness of the forests where beasts reigned supreme were not lacking in the Kingdom of Mewar especially considering there was no more savage and barren land than the Aravalli hills where the Palace of Gogunda was situated and the only living humanity were the rugged Bhils. "Let us go hunting," Udai beckoned to the then young Man Singh.

"Sire, I see no more fitting way to dissuade time from making itself felt." The Maharana thought on his young guest's words.

"Interesting way to express that you don't intend to be bored." The Maharana smiled, "it will take us a season and more to reach the wilderness and indulge in this activity."

"Do you no longer care to see the strength of my arm and the boldness of my heart. Sire? Men that are about you must be tested, must they not?"

"Indeed brother, but you still dwell in the realms of youth."

"Once in the forest, fierce creatures will draw me from this carefree realm into the less pleasant one of manhood, will they not, Sire?"

"I was bargaining on such."

"My youth will accompany me to the world of the unknown spirit, my body is to be used at your service and like iron, tempered by the flames of fire."

It was there, in the depth of the forest that riding beside the Maharana; Man Singh spotted a bull; fierce, hot and not tranquil. "Look Sire," Man Singh cried, "A bull! And it seems to be tied at a stake... how can that be when there is no other man but you and I in the forest?"

"You, yourself are that other man, my friend," the Maharana said looking suspiciously at Man Singh. "What kind of trickery have you employed to tie the bull?"

"I, Sire? I have used no means but my eyes to gaze on the bull that I see now." The bull shook its head wildly and set itself free galloping with speed towards them. The Maharana's horse leaped in the air and bolted with its occupant holding on tightly to its reins and Man Singh pursued the creature until riding side by side, then Man Singh swung onto the bull's spine, grabbing a horn and striking him with his dagger in great depth whence the creature fell to its knees abated. When recovering to the scene, the Maharana still seemed unconvinced. "Some trickery has surely been used, to kill a bull so easily," he said looking at the creature not impressed.

"If you believe it to be so," the young Delwara heir said, "then set me another task."

"Indeed," the Maharana said with surprise at the boldness of his guest. "If you find a bull, free, roaming in the forest and you kill it- then I will declare you a worthy Prince." And that's precisely what happened, this time, the undaunted Man Singh on seeing yet another bull, split the two horns of the creature apart. The Delwara heir, Kunwar Man Singh, was declared a brave Prince and won a prominent position in the Maharana's army during Udai's long and relatively peaceful reign mainly due to the fact that the Muslims were too busy eliminating one another from the Mughal throne. The year was round about 1550.

CHAPTER TWELVE

The Reign of Udai to Preparation for War Against Akbar 1565

Udai offers one of his daughters in marriage to his friend Man of Delwara; Emperor Humayun is reinstated but finds his death shortly afterwards leaving the young Akbar as successor; Udai looks for another Capital fearing Chittor an easy prey to the invaders;Udai's Crown Prince Pratap emerges as somewhat on the wild side; Raja Bhagwan Das of Amber succumbs to a marriage alliance with the Mughal Emperor whose heir General Man Singh will become Pratap's antagonist; Pratap opposes his father giving refuge to Muslim hostages; Man Singh of Delwara's three sons are introduced; the new weapons used by the Mughals are discussed; at the war council against Akbar, Udai entrusts the Mewar gold to his Treasurer Bhama Shah

Even though the Mughal Rulers were busy eliminating one another, they nevertheless, each and everyone one of them had half an eye on Mewar. There was no question that Mewar could not be annexed when it was possible for the rest of India to be so.

On one occasion Udai gathered together his army and met the Afghan invader, Hazi Khan. Alongside the Maharana rode his teenage Crown Prince, Pratap and the faithful Jhala warrior, Man Singh. The Rajputs were at their best and although the battle lasted over three hours and the fighting was intensely ferocious, the Maharana's forces claimed the victory as they watched the Afghan invaders retreat, of which not one had less than five wounds. "And now to celebrate," Udai said tightening his horse's reins, "with a bountiful wedding- yours my faithful Man Sigh- to one of my daughters..." the Maharana smiled. "Choose whichever one you wish; I have eighteen so far..."

Man Singh chose Kushal Kunwar and took her to meet his other wives. Taking the teenage bride by the hand said, "This is Daughter of Kumpawat Rathore…" The first wife bowed and so did Kushal Kunwar. "This is Daughter of Surtan Singh ji," Man Singh stated, "And this is Daughter of Ahadi Sangot Bhopat Singh ji," he continued, "This is Daughter of Dharyawad Ranawat, Daughter of Begu Rawat Narsingh Dewal, Daughter of Jogidas Sara Sarang Devot, and Daughter of Raj Singh Sultan Singh of Baheli Kalyan Pur."

So it was that after a lavish wedding Man Singh became related to the Ruler of Mewar for the second time- not only was the Maharana his brother-in-law, having married Man's sister, but he was now, also Man Singh's father-in-law, since Man Singh was marrying Udai's daughter, not that Man Singh was in any lack of good family ties as can be seen by his list of wives above but obviously, Udai felt a special need to have closer bonds with Man Singh of Delwara.

At the time of Udai's coronation the Sultan, Sher Shah of the Sur Dynasty, who apart from replacing the dam with the rupee had also managed to force the Mughal Emperor Humayun flee and occupy the throne himself. However, Sher Shan's descendant, Shah Sikander II, was overcome by Humayun's twelve year old son Akbar: who against the advice of the Council, Hymayun, allowed to lead the Imperial Army- with glorious effects since he succeeded to reinstate the Mughal Dynasty.

"My trustworthy brother," Udai began as he greeted Man Singh, "My messenger has just brought news from the Imperial Court; Emperor Humayun is dead!"

"Not news expected surely,' Man Singh looked steadily, "the Emperor's reinstatement could not have been shorter… a season, Sire?" The Maharana nodded in agreement. "And the cause, Sire, foul or friendly?"

"Not an easy one to answer is that…" the Maharana hesitated, "I would say accidental… Although six months have passed since he had regained Agra and Delhi from the Sultan, Humayun was still celebrating…" Udai rubbed his moustache with his hand hiding a shrewd smile. "The Emperor was thus engaged with his astrologers on the terrace of his Mahal… drinking wine, smoking pipes of opium…"

"And Sire?"

"He heard the *muezzin* summoning the hour of prayer… He was going down the steps…" another smile crept across the Maharana's lips, "he knelt down to pray- but he was so drunk he did not notice there was step at the top of the stairs- he fell all the way down and broke his skull."

"And now we have a thirteen year old Emperor on the throne of Delhi," Pratap, Udai's first born said. "Was I not born only two years further back in time than Akbar, father?"

"Precisely..." Udai paused, "Now don't you start getting ideas about becoming Maharana of Mewar before your time!" Udai raised his index finger as he spoke. "I'm not going to die for some time yet..."

"With the help of the gods, Sire," Man Singh interrupted.

"Of course," the Maharana said rubbing his moustache, "And you will see to that, naturally." Man Singh bowed respectfully in answer. "But now let us go into this matter of the Mughal Dynasty that Akbar has established, thirteen years old or not, he is determined to be here to stay," Udai stated, then turning faced Man Singh directly. "Is Chittor," the Maharana pouted ironically, "where we are now, not upon a hill, my valiant Jhala Rajput?"

"And such an easy prey for the enemy, Sire?"

"All Akbar has to do," Pratap said intervening, "is cut off the food supplies..."

"Precisely!" Udai exclaimed dryly. "It's time to move house."

It was during his 19th year as Ruler of Mewar, while on a thanksgiving pilgrimage for the birth of his grandson, to the god Eklingji, south west of Chittor that Udai saw what he wanted. The tall hills of Gogunda and Kumbhalgarh overlooked the valley, he sensed the beauty of the forest, the river and the land enchanted him. "This is where I shall make my new Capitol faithful Man Singh," he said while Pratap the Crown Prince looked on. "This is a contrast to Chittor and as Akbar's hand urges for steel, Mughal steps will seek to plunder that hill again."

"Father," Pratap said turning to the Maharana, "It is my belief that the Arvalli Hills above, will serve us best."

"In time of war you may need to withdraw even further than Gogunda, to your birth place Kumbhalgarh... but in peace time we need sweet and pleasant lands for surely we are royal princes are we not?"

"Kumbhalgarh is a distance we cannot reach in time to save our skins..." the sultry Pratap halted, "Gogunda rather... is a kingdom aloof..." Pratap uttered prophetically- "we can get out but they can't come in!"

"You are fast learning the strategies of war," the Maharana said placing a hand on his son's shoulder. "The Delhi Emperor will not catch you unaware... and as he can't get you that way, he will contrive to seek a marriage alliance with you."

"Akbar may try to convince other Rajputs to give their daughters, sisters, cousins and aunts to a Muslim," Pratap paused shrewdly, "Though I believe without success so far…"

"That may not be for long," Udai interrupted, "Intelligence has disclosed to me that the House of Amber is about to succumb…"

"Raja Bhagwan Das!" Pratap said astonished. "He has always been one of our most trustworthy alliances…"

"You can forget that now, I believe Humayun had arranged for the sister of Raja Bhagwan Das of Amber to marry Akbar…"

"Another child marriage!" Man Singh interrupted. "These Muslims go around preaching that our practise of seeing our youngsters paired off before they can walk as unethical and then… right under our noses they arrange marriage alliances between them and our allies with an offspring who has hardly been weaned from his mother's breasts, let alone reached the age of reason."

"You can't really say that Akbar has just been weaned from his mother's breast, honourable Man Singh," Pratap said, "as I had reminded my father, my own birth was only two years further back in time the birth of Akbar… and am I not a man?"

"The way you handle that sword," Man Singh answered slowly, "made you a warrior long before you became a man."

"I thought being a man was being a warrior," Pratap paused, "Don't the two go together?"

"Not always," Man Singh placed a hand upon the boy's shoulders, "I was a man before I became a warrior…"

"Your thoughts were always high above- among the gods," Udai intervened. "And your eyes saw pictures of events that were no where near from where you were placed…"

"How remarkable to see visions," Pratap said, "if I could do that, I would be able to see which battlefield Akbar was heading for next…"

"Don't be blasphemous!" Udai warned, "Gifts from the gods must not be tampered with."

"You, yourself Sire, forced me to be a warrior," Man Singh reminded.

"Indeed," Udai said with a huge smile savouring moments of past mischief, "making you kill a second bull pretending that you had killed the first by trickery and not by your own efforts…"

"I had sensed you were testing my faithfulness, Sire."

"You were not stupid! But a ruler must know the men who stand around him- see them with transparency..." the Maharana paused, "I must admit I had no difficulty in seeing through you at all- you are as clear as a raindrop."

"I thank you Sire," Man Singh bowed, "but one person whom I suspect will find difficulty in passing the transparency test is the son of Raja Bhagwan Das, who, much to my misfortune possesses my own same name."

"And my own same day, month and year of birth..." Pratap intervened.

"Consequently," Man Singh interrupted, "name and birth crossed with the House of Mewar, the destiny of Man Singh of Amber must be entwined with ours."

"Whose father has traded his own sister- flesh from his own parents flesh- for a footstool in the Mughal Empire, is nothing less than a traitor!" Pratap said angrily.

"His career in the Mughal Army is already defined..."

"He had best not set foot on Mewar soil," Pratap answered.

"Now, son," Udai interrupted, "a touch of diplomacy with these Mughals is never wasted... for theirs is the power and much of it too."

"Not in Mewar they have not and never will have!" Pratap swore, then as if recalling something, turned towards the Maharana, "But you father," he said slowly, "are not much of a diplomatic gentleman are you?"

"Meaning son?"

"Chittor is full of refugees, royal as they may be but still Muslims they are..."

"Some shrewdness must be used, my son," Udai paused, "some day they may be of use..."

"Hostages then?"

"I wouldn't go as far as that," Udai's eyes rolled upwards nonchalantly, "I would prefer to describe the matter as a question of forced hospitality- more as a token, for a pledge of course."

"What sort of a pledge?" Pratap asked.

"When they get their kingdom back, they leave us alone... a favour always deserves a favour..."

"Not always does that occur..." Pratap gazed downwards.

"But let us not talk of war..." Udai interjected, "it is a moment for cheer and of thanks: let us therefore render due homage to the god of

Eklingji for granting a third generation heir to the throne of Mewar- the son of my own son- Amar."

"I give you thanks, father," Pratap said, then turned towards Man Singh of Delwara, "your eyes see beyond those of men, they see in the holiness of the gods, intercede therefore, well loved Man Singh, that the gods grant my son a love for those hills, make him a Spartan prince and not a lover of comfort and finesse."

"Fathers can make their sons like themselves no more than sons can make fathers like them," Man Singh said glancing at the Maharana whose refined metal shared little with the ruggedness of his son.

"If it pleases you son," Udai said, "you may well live in the wilderness of the hills, but a royal Prince must not only be so in name but also appear to be what he is- and that requires a kingdom- a lavish and splendid kingdom as it will be when I build my capital on this genteel and tender land."

"I prefer to have my shoulders well guarded by Rana Punja..." The Crown Prince paused, "now, there's a man whose naked torso has never felt the touch of silk or whose lisps has never savoured sweet meats..."

"The Ruler of the mountain Bhils has by tradition been the faithful protector of the Mewar throne," Man Singh added.

"A man whom you will never see in a darbar court!" Pratap affirmed, "but who will stealthily mingle with the forest animals so the enemy can never distinguish man from beast..."

"If the enemy ever gets that far," Man Singh's brother Bhopat said as he presented himself to the Maharana with two of Man Singh's young sons, Kalyan and Asoji. "Rana Punja has the Arvalli passes guarded by fifteen thousand arrows- It is not an easy feat to cross those hills from Delwara and not be taken for the enemy," Bhopat concluded. The two boys stepped forwards and greeted their father. "And where is my other son, Shatrusal?" Man Singh asked.

"At the end of the procession with our noble grandfather," the slightly taller one, Kalyan, said. Udai flashed a smile of pleasure and said,

"Your noble grandfather is here? It will be a joyous occasion to see Rana Jait- we shall all return to Chittogarh and prepare arms to gain the North East territories," Udai paused and turned to the two Jhala brothers, "Do you know what in the battle of Khanwa blew up my father, the Great Rana Sanga's arse?

"Balls! Gunpowder balls, Sire!" The voice from a distance came closer.

"Raja Jait! You old scoundrel," the Maharana said with delight as he greeted Man Singh's father, "about time you showed up."

"That's how my uncle Ajja was blown to pieces as he was carrying the Royal standard for your father, the wounded great Sanga," Jait said. Then turning to the younger boy beside him, Asoji, added, "Take heed young man, that's how the brave die."

"My grandfather too?" Asoji asked.

"I am your grandfather!" Jait's eyes widened.

"I mean the one before you, grandfather Sajja."

"Your own father's death at the 2nd Sack of Chittor was even more gruesome than that of his brother, was it not?" Udai intervened addressing himself to Jait, "At least your uncle Ajja died decently, honourably, I would say..."

"Yes, uncle Ajja by donning the Great Maharana Sanga's cloak died a hero..." Jait said.

"Apart from that," Udai continued, waving his hand as if to dismiss the matter lightly, "your uncle Ajja died quite conventionally, arrows and things like that..." Udai paused, "Whereas, your father, the unfortunate Sajja was blown to kingdom come with those immoral Portuguese contraptions... what are they called... fireworks..."

"Gunpowder, Sire," Man Singh interrupted. "Times have changed. Our fathers fought with swords, lances and arrows..."

"But the Muslims have imported those contraptions from those meddling Europeans..." Udai began, "The Portuguese, I was told they are called... Akbar is not sleeping... always keeping himself updated," he looked at the nobles around him, "And do you know what for?"

"Yes father," his son Pratap volunteered, "to blow up, in turn, our own arses too."

"Then the sooner we change house the better- We will start construction of the new capital here, this very day!" Udai turned around and added with a tone of surprise, "What day is it?"

"The year is 1559 Sire," Jait offered, "but as to the day..." he shook his head.

"It is the season after my son's birth..." Pratap said, "We celebrated the birth of Amar at Chittor for many days in Spring- Amar was born in spring... so it is summer now."

"And the day?" Udai insisted. But as no one knew what day it was that day, the exact date of the founding of the City of Udaipur was never recorded.

As the excavations for a smaller lake next to the one existing began in the new capital, at Chittor the elders of the Mewar court gathered with great frequency. Things were not going at all well for Mewar with the new Emperor. Thirteen years, he may have been when Akbar became Emperor, now, he was a few years older and even more determined than ever to take possession of the whole of Rajputana- all Rajputs under his Imperial command- that had been Akbar's dream from childhood. But now he was no longer a child and in the meantime he had managed to confirm the work begun by his father Humayn; the Rao of Amber and his son, General Man Singh of Amber were well under the young Emperor's control. The court at Mewar looked on with disgust.

"A Rajput! A son of our own gods has become a general in Akbar's army…" Pratap stormed as he flung open the doors of the men's quarters. "A Rajput in the Muslim Army!" The ill awaited news echoed through all passageways of the palace in Chittorgarh.

"A Rajput General, even if in the Muslim army would never kill his own kindred- Hindus like himself," Maharana Udai said with a certain calm that only irritated his son even more. "What do you say Noble Raja Jait, you who seem to hop from one court to another as if it were a game."

"Your Majesty," Jait began, "You know my cause for joining the forces of Marwar, I have more than one son and Delwara is not enough for both."

"Never mind such trifles," Udai said waving his hand irritably. "I am sure my Crown Prince will concede one of his jagir's to your son Man Singh…"

"Provided he pays the Nazrana," Pratap intervened quickly while the Maharana ignored his son's outburst. Udai rubbed his hand over his curved moustache.

"Which jagir?" he said pensively, Mandalgarh…? No, too close to Amber and to that traitor Rajput General… Let's see. Ah, I know just the place," Udai said suddenly, "Gogunda!"

"Gogunda!" Pratap said horrified. "That father, you cannot do! I was brought up in Gogunda, I know every tuft of earth, every grain of soil, and I am able to call each of the fifteen thousand Bhils by name."

"We need the money son!" Udai said astutely in Pratap's ear. "Jait is a warrior and has won many battles for the Rao of Marwar so he has money in his purse- and we need money if we are to stave off Akbar from taking

Chittor," Udai concluded slipping away from his son's side. "But let's now return to the question in hand, Raja Jait, your opinion on the General."

"Sire, be he a Rajput or no, Man Singh of Amber is a Mughal General..."

"Yes, yes Raja Jait," Udai said waving his hand impatiently, "you are telling us nothing new."

"What I was about to say, Sire, if it is conceded for me to conclude the matter, the General in question be he Rajput or no he has no scruples in annihilating one of his fellow Hindus."

"Why say you thus?" the Maharana asked.

"The Imperial forces, headed by this General from Amber, have set fire to a number of villages around Mewar's Ranthanbhor and killed hordes of Hindus.

"You bring bad tidings Raja Jait. By attacking Ranthanbhor, neutralizing our stronghold in Amber, is nothing less than a declaration of war," Pratap said hotly.

"Intelligence tells me," Jait continued, that Akbar is assembling his army ready to march...

"On Chittor, of course," Udai said troubled, "he has taken all the other kingdoms, even Malwa, the great Malwa..."

"Talking of Malwa," Pratap's voice had a sinister tone, "since you've broght up the subject, father, allow me to remind you that the scoundrel you have running around the palace as presumably a 'guest' is none other than Baz Bahadur- a Sultan- not a Rajput... You are giving hospitality to an Afghan, a foreigner, not one of our kind."

"I forsee the Sultan back on the throne of Malwa as soon as we have ousted Akbar from Chittor and as you know son... a favour always deserves a favour..."

"Is the past not warning enough for you father... The first sack of Chittor came about because Ratan gave hospitality to a Sultan- And your own father too, my grandfather Sangram fell at Khanwa for the same reason..."

"Not always does that occur..." Udai said calmly, "it is better to have a friend on the throne of Malwa rather than an enemy." Pratap gazed downwards, not convinced of his father's words.

"Malwa was a Rajput stronghold once..."

"It is mindful enough that we hang on to our own throne here in Mewar, son, is it not?" His son made no answer.

"Sire," Jait said pointing down to the road below at the foot of the tower, "Look, the chiefs from Badnore, from Marwar, from Jodhpur, from the whole of the kingdom are arriving- they have come to defend Chittor, their capitol."

"Father, we must assemble..."

"Call all the elders, nobles, generals and open the war council," Udai ordered. "Above all call the Treasurer, the noble Bhama Shah," Udai stopped his Chieftain, "in private, I want to see the Prime Minister here, alone."

When Bhama Shah entered the private quarters of the Maharana, Udai bade him to sit close in front of him so that he could speak in low tones which would not be carried from beyond their ears. "I have a vital assignment to inflict upon you, my faithful Prime Minister."

"You have only to speak, Sire," Bhama Shah said bowing low his head in acceptance.

"This very hour you will take two thirds of the Mewar gold to a place of safety in the Aravalli hills where only you have knowledge," the Maharana rose in anger, "I do not want those Mughals to get their greedy hands on it," his look became foreboding. "Should I not survive the attack on Chittor..."

"Sire, you will not be permitted to stay in Chittor, the council will compel you to repair to Kumbhalgarh..."

"Indeed not!"

"But Sire, what use is a kingdom with its head severed?"

"There will be another head."

"His Highness Crown Prince Pratap will also not be allowed to stay..."

"No war council is going to stop that hot headed son of mine from fighting for Chittor."

"That may be so, but the Council will enforce Prince Pratap to lead the second force that will disrupt the Mughal supplies from the Aravalli hills, if the Royal Prince must fight at all."

"Yes, he must, no question of that- the only way he may be prevented from fighting is by chaining him to the dungeon bars."

"If the case is so, then the Council will submit to the Royal wishes. Bhama Shah, Mewar's proven Rajput warrior looked astutely at the Maharana. "But you Sire, permit me to say, have knowledge from your days of youth that discretion is preferable to valour."

"I will not take second place in the attack against Akbar!" Pratap bellowed in front of the Assembly.

"Enough!" the Maharana intervened. "Either you take command in the Aravalli hills or the dungeon!" Udai commanded, "The Line of Mewar must be preserved."

"Father, you have twenty five sons!"

"But only one Crown Prince!"

"Sire!" Jaimal of Badnore, one of the young genrals cried, "News comes that the Emperor himself, Akbar, is leading a full Imperial army towards Chittor…"

"And the false Rajput Genral Man Sign is at his side," Patta, another general from the Sisodia house of Amet," added quickly. "It is a six kilometre strong army Sire!"

"Sire! Make haste, you must retire to Gogunda- Our second army await you in the Arvalli hills!" the elder of the Chieftains admonished. The Maharana stepped down, then said mournfully, "And may the gods have mercy!"

CHAPTER THIRTEEN

War Strategies of the 3rd Sack of Chittor by Akbar 1567-8

The Rajput Generals Jaimal and Patta

Udai and his Crown Prince arrived in Gogunda only days before Akbar settled his army in a space that covered six kilometres on the plains below the hundred and twenty two metres high fortress of Chittor. It was the 25th day of October in the year of 1567 when the green banner of Islam was seen flying in the encampment that Akber had swiftly set up.

Not satisfied with that he wanted his presence to be even further noticed so he erected a ten metre high column in the shape of a pyramid which, granted, was not even a tenth of the fortress that towered above him and in comparison a modest show of the Imperial power which Akbar considered omnipotent, however he had to be satisfied with such for the time being until of course, he would take possession of this Rajput tower of supremacy which he was intent on annihilating. Placing a lamp on the peak of this pyramid would let the world know that he, Akbar, the Imperial Emperor was there and that would be enough to discourage any kind of interference from outsiders. This of course meant no one could enter the fortress, neither friend nor foe, armed by its eight thousand strong Rajput guardians, which also meant once supplies had depleted, the eight thousand warriors inside Chittor would starve to death.

However, supplies, wells and reservoirs inside the fortress were plentiful, nor could the Imperial soldiers enter to poison the water as it was possible in Kumbhalgarh above Gogunda in the Arvalli hills and had been the cause of many battles lost by Rajputs. But just as Akbar stopped the possibility of supplies entering Chittorgarh, the Maharana and his

Crown Prince, Pratap boycotted the supplies from the north which would necessitate pass through Gogunda and its surroundings, thus food nor ammunition could ever reach Akbar. Swiftness, time was imperative. It was time more than ammunitions that would be the determining factor of who should win or lose. Akbar, even more so than the Rajputs knew this, having no intentions of bowing to time and become its slave- he would conquer time and time would be his slave. This he would achieve with the aid of his knowledge of engineering.

Akbar skilfully placed his forces around the fortress, cannons encircled it and an impenetrable blockade was formed and for months he shelled against the fortress but not even cannon firing had any significant effect against the immense walls. Besides, Jaimal and the other young Generals were quick to repair overnight, whatever damage had been made. Akbar charged the walls with violence, but nothing crumbled. Any of his cavalry or warriors endeavouring to enter the winding roadways were hit immediately by the sharpshooters on the ramparts. No one could climb its heights, stopped by the huge gates and colossal strongholds. The Rajputs were relentless and Akbar closely escaped death more than once. It was at this point, with time against him that the Emperor experienced the first realizations of a power superior to his own- that of the fortress of Chittor. But the Emperor had only one intent- to vanquish Rajput power in Mewar for ever and that meant to obliterate Chittor completely as a landmark in Rajputana.

Not closing an eye but crafting a way to bring his intent to fruition the Emperor sought the weaker part of the fortifications- for everywhere, in every place, there is one part which is not as strong as the rest. The southern end of the Fort showed itself to be not as high, there he build his famed Mohur Magri so called since to every basket of soil that each soldier brought Akbar gave a golden coin- a mohur thus stimulating his warriors to work harder and build the mount even higher. This mount upon which Akbar intended to place his cannons took months to build but as this plan too made little if any damage he placed landmines but Jaimal's counter attacks destroyed in great part the elite of the Imperial Army. Literally thousands of corpses of the Emperor's officers and engineers strewed the encampment. But Akbar was able to find a use for his best men even after death and used them to erect walls to create the 'sabats' (sheltered roadways) so as to besiege the fortress under the cover of protection from the defensive. In other words the Imperial army was erecting a fortress upon another fortress with the remains of their dead.

In spite of the bullet proof roofs that protected the Imperial constructers, the Rajput artillery and horsemen killed at least one hundred workers every day; nevertheless, shortly the sabats reached the same height as the walls of the Fort itself. The sabats were mined with gunpowder and a special place on one of the roofs was set aside so that the Emperor could view the proceeds of the battle. The first mine which was set off blew up one of the bastions and the Mughals dashed through the gap with wild cries as they were met with the onslaught of the Rajputs. For some reason, obviously a mistake, the second mine exploded and sent everyone to smithereen for miles around. The attack continued for two nights but to no avail, Akbar had to retreat. He was however more resolute than ever to take the fort in one way or another so as to leave a sign that in future, no fortress would ever hold out against him- never again.

He pushed the damaged sabat forward, then he positioned himself on top with his matchlock gun and there he paraded every night and fired at every light he spied inside the fort. As every night, Jaimal would go up the bastions, to ensure his men had done a good job on the repairs, eventually, Akbar figured out that this was the man he was seeking, the General in charge of Chittor. That was Akbar's main target- to destroy the leader. As always Akbar was on the look out on top of the sabat and his chance came that very night. The stealthy figure of Jaimal crept up the bastion, a light suddenly lit up the figure which Akbar recognized as that of a Rajput and fired without failing the mark, even in the dark. The ball of fire shattered Jaimal's thigh and as he lay dispirited he insisted that the resistance should continue immediately appointing the young Patta from Amet as Commander- surrender was not negotiable ever.

After four months of relentless battle, supplies were beginning to get short on both sides. To Akbar this meant that the end of Chittor was in sight since in one way or another he would always be able to get supplies of some sort from the north in spite of Udai's querrilla attacks in the Arvalli pass, but not the Rajputs, the Rajputs were completely cut off. Thus, supposedly, it was to spare further grovelling on the camp and get home to his Imperial comforts as soon as possible, that Akbar sent word he was willing to negotiate a peace treaty, meaning surrender of course, which he immediately thought Patta would accept- starvation was at the door and escape non-existent. Patta sent his two most able nobles, they too, scarcely older than the teenage General. The negotiations at the Mughal camp came to no agreement. The Emperor insisted that he would be emperor of the whole of Mewar sooner or later and it was senseless holding out since the rest of the region was under his command- there remained only the Maharana of Udaipur and once Chittor, his headquarters was vanquished, which, Akbar warned was only a matter of days, what would become of the Maharana?

The Emperor, painting a picture so black of the prospects of Rajputana did not in any way deter the two young Rajputs- rather they were willing to be slaughtered on the field than be slaves of the Mughal Emperor. Akbar knew victory for him was at hand, one way or the other. He had hoped in submission rather than slaughter but a Rajput would prefer slaughter to submission. Nevertheless, Akbar admired the courage and unconditional loyalty of these young nobles, preferring them a hundred times over to his own warriors whom in order to put in their best efforts he always had to dangle the carrot in front of them and pay out gold coins non stop. Hence, the Emperor made a concession, a special favour, just to show his amiability, he would concede them a Hindu funeral, cremate them when dead.

On February 24th 1568, when there was not a scrap of food to eat or ammunition to fire, the lumber was piled up and oil poured over it. The nine queens, five princes and all other females in the palace were placed on top, set fire to and perished throughout the whole of that day. The next day, as soon as a flicker of light crept across the sky, clad in saffron, the Rajputs threw open the gates and carrying the bleeding Jaimal shoulder high fell unto the front line of the firing squad of the Imperial army that awaited them along the roadway. On seeing Jaimail carried thus shouder high by his cousin, Akbar thought he had a vision of the god Vishnu as the four arms holding immense swords came towards him.

Jaimal's cousin was quickly beheaded and the falling Jaimal was pierced through with a sword. Akbar then sent in the war elephants, one of which whisked Patta with his trunk, smashed him to the floor and trampled him underfoot. The Imperial soldiers then flooded into every byway, quarter, lane, building and even temple, killing, slaughtering, beheading, and crushing every living presence in sight. Akbar then mounting his horse, strode majestically through the empty, devastated ruins of what was the grandeur of Mewar, being he, the total and complete Conqueror.

CHAPTER FOURTEEN

At the Court of Delwara and birth of Udaipur

Jait is killed at the 3ʳᵈ Sack of Chittor, investiture of his son Man Singh as Raja; personality clash between Udai and his Crown Prince Pratap, Udai's preference for younger son Jagmal; Udai continues to construct his new headquarters on the Pichola Lake while Pratap withdraws to Gogunda; personality clash between Pratap and his own son Amar; the death of Udai

The gates to Delwara sprang open as the royal figure on horseback came hurtling across the plain with his retinue of mountain warriors, the Bhils, following. Solem tones of music coming from the Throne Room of Delwara echoed in the courtyard. Pratap dismounted, placed an affectionate hand over wide forehead and large eyes of his white stallion, Chetak, stroke its short neck gently before letting the Bhils take it, not allowing the guards to handle it. The Crown Prince strode towards the main entrance alone when his father Maharana Udai stepped into the courtyard alongside his Prime Minister, Bhama Shah and the Maharana's ninth and favourite son Jagmal. Pratap knew he had missed the Talwar[36] ceremony of his father's bosom friend and brother-in-law, having married one of the sisters of Man Singh of Delwara whose father Jait had fallen that same year under Akbar's attack at Chittor and he Man Singh himself having married one of Udai's daughters.

"Your are late son!" Udai said disaproovingly. Pratap made an attempt at a decent salutation. Jagmal looking on with an air of superiority coming from the awareness of being protected by their royal father said:

---

36 Ceremony of the sword some time after a newly enthroned sovereign

"Indeed brother, they are at the gift exchange stage…"

"And what did you give our noble Raja Man Singh…" Pratap had barely asked when their father interrupted:

"Quite, what did we get, Shah Bhama?" Udai said indicating a red purse held by his Prime Minister.

"Rather meagre entrance," the Prime Minister said holding up the velvet pouch. "But since Raja Man Singh has created a delightful garden and built a Zardana in Gogunda Palace, it is compensation enough, is it not?"

"Compensation?" Pratap bemused, "for building a male's quarters in a fortress? I would have thought that's the least you could expect from its occupiers…" he paused. "As for the garden… what use have I for shady trees to walk in when I have the Aravalli forests?"

"Do not expect any finesse of mind from our Crown Prince, dear Prime Minister!" Udai muttered displeased.

"Having all been wiped clean by Akbar's forces, the whole of Mewar is grovelling…" the Prime Minister said, "besides, Man Singh has only been granted the Jagir of Delwara without Gogunda…"

"If you hadn't insisted in keeping Gogunda for yourself," the Maharana said turning to Pratap, "we would have had that extra revenue…" The Maharana took a closer look at his son almost in disgust. "How a noble Prince can possibly grovel around the Arvalli hills of Gogunda with a retinue of wild Bhils around him is beyond my comprehension."

"The Arvalli's have saved us from sure slaughter and they will continue to prevent Akbar from setting his hands on you my dear father, and I your Crown Prince!" Pratap waved his hand impatiently, "Instead of spending our depleted resources on building a new headquarters we should concentrate on getting Chittor back!" Pratap's anger could not be hidden- "I swear," he continued, "I will not shave this beard ever again," he pulled at the dark unkept hair under his chin, "until Chittor is regained!" He paused only momentarily to show his earnestness, "Nor will I eat from golden plates again…"

"Does that mean we must ask Raja Man Singh to serve your food on leaves?" Jagmal asked brashly.

"Precisely!" Pratap answered ignoring his brother's impudence. "I will not rest until Chittor is mine again!"

"Indeed!" the Maharana said smoothly curling his moustache around his forefinger. "Yours, you say?" Udai's eyes narrowed as he looked directly as his Crown Prince. "Sometimes I wonder if you are fit to reign after me. Just look at the state of your condition- appearing at the crowning ceremony of my dearest of all neighbours looking as if you have been just dragged out of the forest- you have no semblance of a Royal Prince."

"The veneer of Princes is not of my taste father and my presence here is simply to endorse Man Singh on the throne of Delwara."

"In that case," Udai answered, "your duty here is in excess since I as Maharana of Mewar is abundance enough to endorse Man Singh as Raja of Delwara." Udai then turned to his younger son Jagmal and beckoned, "Let us repair inside and leave your half-brother to the wilderness of the Aravallis."

"Think again father," Pratap called, "before building your City Palace at the Pichola Lake, the fogliage and ruggedness of the Aravalli's may be of aid to you even yet."

As Pratap walked away towards the stables, some of the guests were coming out into the courtyard into the heat of the sun on their way to the roof-top where the meal had been set, among them were Kalyn and Shatrushal, the two elder sons of Man Singh.

"Was that not your brother the noble Kunwar[37] Pratap?" Shatrushal asked Jagmal as he neared the royal group.

"Linger not after him," Udai said promptly, "I've sent him off for a wash!" Shatrushal smiled at the Maharan's attempt at being witty.

"I regret not to have had the honour of speaking with him, Sire."

"You have lost nothing, Shatrushal- he is like an elephant with a sore head."

"Because of Akbar, I vouch."

"You vouch right…"

"My sword is at his service…"

"Whose service?" The Maharana asked gamely, "Akbar's…"

"Indeed you jest, Sire."

"Indeed, I do, but it would not surprise me if you too strayed into that direction, Pratap's brother, my own son, Sakta has joined Akbar's ranks." Udai shook his head- "always had been a troublesome child- I even condemned him to death, once!"

"Father, he was only five!" Jagmal interrupted.

"That was my mistake, I should have executed him there and then, not wait to banish him years later for causing the death of our venerable family priest."

---

37 Prince- title given to the son of a living sovereign

"But wasn't that our brother Pratap's fault? Wasn't he who proposed a challenge of the lance, to the last blood?"

"It matters not whose fault it was, they were always at each other's throat and since one of them had to go- it had to be the younger," Udai turned to Jagmal, "and again that was a mistake, sometimes younger sons are better Princes..." the Maharana shook his head, "but who can tell... I had no son worse than Sakta- not even Pratap," he said in attempt to assure himself he had made the right choice. And as the guests were becoming numerous in the courtyard, the Maharana led the procession to the rooftop.

Of course, Udai took no heed of his Crown Prince's admonitions of holding the Aravalli hills more dear and continued with relentless vigour to construct his new headquarters beside the Pichola Lake south in the Aravallis which permitted him to live in the luxury that his rank required and unreachable enough for the enemy not to move in unannounced. In the meantime Pratap continued with equal relentless vigour to oust Akbar from as much of Mewar's soil as possible and regain much of what had been taken... much that is- except Chittorgarh.

During this period it was difficult either to find the Maharana, his Crown Prince or even Mewar's headquarters. Pratap had made his abode at Gogunda Palace that he alternated with the fotress of Kumbhalgarh above, which went even deeper into the Aravalli's. The Maharana was more often than not to be found beside the Pichola Lake costructing the new headquarters of Mewar, which when done he would name the city wherein it was contained, Udaipur, after himself.

In 1570, although the workers' huts were still assembled, as construction of the numerous facets of the new Royal Palace were still in progress, Udai settled in the new City Palace and declared it Mewar's new headquarters. Pratap had no intention of obliging his father and moving in, from Gogunda, the Crown Prince would not be moved. A summons was promptly delivered to the erring Crown Prince to remove himself and his household, in particular Pratap's first born, Amar, to repair to the City Palace in the newfound city of Udaipur.

The coming together was not a happy occasion since Pratap saw nothing to celebrate when Chittorgarh was still bleeding in his enemy's hands. All the delicate finesse, embroidery, precious stones, materials and decorations repulsed the rugged senses used to sleeping in animal dens, feeding upon wild berries and communicating with sounds and signs only known to the mountain savages.

As soon as the formalities with his father were over, Pratap went across to where the workers' huts were still assembled, taking his own son Amar who was not too happy with the idea of messing around with the cow dung and mud making of the builders. Amar complained to his father on the insistence of actually going inside the huts to see just how the other side lived.

"Is it really necessary father?" the youth said as he tapped the dust off his elbow which he procured while accidently rubbing against a board. "What can I possibly learn inside this dark hole?" Pratap said nothing. He then bent down and grovelled in the earth like a savage. "Father!" the boy cried.

"This and much more, you must do," Pratap said digging his nails in the ground, "you must learn to subject your body to your will, if you are to rule a kingdom."

"Grandfather doesn't do that and he's the Maharana!"

"Grandfather has lost Chittor! And I must regain it- and you don't regain a kingdom sitting on velvet cushion as you so want to do."

"But I'm a Prince…"

"You are the guardian, the guardian of Mewar- or you will be when I'm gone!" With that Pratap pulled himself up from the ground and made his way out with the youth close at his heels, but forgetting to bend his head, Amar caught his turban on one of the bamboo reeds holding up the doorway which sent his turban flying to the floor. Amar, annoyed at the happening cursed for the inconvenience, which perturbed his father. "If you become aggravated by such small things son, how will you withstand, the torture, famine, imprisonment and derision of the Mughals?"

And so it was that from that day on, in spite of the temptation of the ease and comfort of the sumptuous City Palace in Udaipur, Amar was always at his father's side in battle and regained even more lands that had been taken by Akbar- more lands yes, but not Chittor. However, in spite of having made of Amar a valiant warrior, almost like himself, Pratap still had some misgiving that Amar once Maharana would concede himself the life of easiness he had aspired in youth. But Pratap's misgiving was nothing to the unease that Udai had towards making Pratap his own successor; in effect, the Maharana had other plans.

Since it was quite an enterprise to get Pratap to attend upon the Maharana at Udaipur, the Maharana repaired to Gogunda, the excuse being a hunting trip with Man Singh of Delwara. Yet, although Udai was not yet fifty that February of 1572, he did not feel in shape to go hunting and on the last day of that month he lay dying surrounded by his elders and favourite wife, Rani Bhatiyani, mother of Jagmal. The Rani insisted on remaining close to his bed-side and continuously whispered in the Maharana's ear, much to the displeasure of the surrounding dignitaries. The Choodawat from Salumber Krishna Das nudged Akhey Raj Songara who was the father of Pratap's mother and said "Don't you think your daughter should be here, after all she is the Maharana's first wife?"

"Indeed," Akhey answered, "but she is also the eldest and the Maharana has long sought other pastures for his pleasure," he nodded towards Udai's favourite by his bedside, Rani Bhatiyani.

"What on earth, has she got to whisper about that she could not have whispered before?"

"Her suit for her son as successor, no doubt," Man Singh of Delwara intervened.

"Jagmal! To lead us in battle with Akbar at our doorstep waiting to pounce- heaven forbid!" Man Singh objected. At that point Udai beckoned his Prime Minister to come near and with an ailing voice pronounced Jagmal as his successor. Pratap took a step forward but Akhey Songara put forth his hand and stepped forward himself.

"Sire, Crown Prince Pratap is your lawful heir."

"My Crown Prince," Udai whispered, "would make you all eat off oak leaves at his own coronation!" He paused and waved his hand as if to put an end to the matter, "Jagmal looks much nicer sitting on a throne!"

So it was that at the funeral of Udai, Pratap did not stay behind in order to be crowned Maharana as the custom decreed the throne should not be left empty, but he followed the funeral procession leaving Jagmal behind to be enthroned. However, the elders were having none of it and left Jagmal sitting on the throne alone, procrastinated the ceremony until the return of Pratap then asked Jagmel to kindly remove his posterior from the throne and sit opposite, the place where younger brothers were to sit. Indignant, Jagmal flatly refused claiming his father had nominated him heir, never mind if he was born first second or third! At that point Akhey Raj Songara and the Choodawat Krishna Das took hold of the chirpy Prince, each on either side, lifted him from the throne and removed his presence from the ceremony, to where, it is not known. What is known is that in revenge, Jagmal promptly joined the ranks of Akbar who awaited him with open arms appointing him ruler of Sirohi, the place of which had been left empty by the death of the Emperor's father-in-law. Of course, Jagmal was not among strangers since another son of Udai, the one the

Maharana had once sentenced to death at the age of five, Sakta, had long joined the Mughal ranks. And surely enough they had much news, and lots more, to exchange.

CHAPTER FIFTEEN

At the Court of the Great Akbar

Akbar's conversation with Pratap's exiled brother, Sakta; Akbar gives his Rajput General Man Singh of Amber a mission

In spite of the horrific sack of Chittorgarh in 1567 Patrap, for the sake of a quiet life, had not once thought of becoming a part of the Mughal Empire. On the contrary, his mind was always churning out how he could protect Mewar from being annexed. For a few years after the events of Chittor, Akbar left Mewar well alone since he was busy elsewhere, his attention was taken up in capturing Gujarat, and secondly, in keeping the newly conquered Malwa in the south-east, under his control.

But in about 1573, just one year after the enthronement of Pratap as 54th Ruler of Mewar, Akbar was getting restless.

"Where is that Savage that calls himself Maharana?" Akbar exploded to his Navratnas[38] as another of his emissary to the court of Mewar returned empty handed.

"At his capital, I should suggest to your Majesty," Birbal, he, who had been selected as one of the court's elders for his renowned wit, remarked. Akbar was silent and then turned with his usual patience to face the speaker as he poured some wine into his goblet:

"At his capital, indeed Birbal... What capital?" the Emperor whispered to him ironically. Birbal's gaze turned serious. "Because if you remember rightly, we took the last capital of Mewar, six years ago, did we not? Is Chittor not our conquest or am I mistaken?" Akbar placed the wine goblet to his lips. Birbal continued to look serious and then grinned as if enlightened by an unexpected streak of genius-

"Udaipur? Your Majesty, the new Capital is Udaipur."

---

38 "Nine Jewels" denoting the nine elders of Akbar's court

"That was his father's capital, Pratap has never set foot on those grounds…"

"Lake, your Majesty…" Akbar looked quizzically at his chief wit booster. "The Maharana's new Palace is on a lake, Lake Pichola."

"Am I supposed to be amused?" Akbar said down in the mouth, "the next we'll hear is that the Maharana can walk on water- just like Jesus Christ!"

"Who?" Raja Man Singh, his general, asked.

"No one you would know, being a Hindu…" Abul-Fazel, Akbar's biographer said. Akbar looked cross-eyed at his biographer.

"Does that imply that only Muslims like myself have insight into Christianity?"

"In reality" Abul-Fazel began, "your Majesty succumbs to no faith but his own…"

"And not even to that!" Akbar was prompt to reply, he poured more wine in his goblet… "for I am a god to myself…"

"What ever that may mean…" Birbal sprung up.

"Don't push your luck too far!" Akbar said laughing, "otherwise you may find yourself back in that muck pool I fished you out from, besides, my religion is reserved only for a select few."

"And I am grateful to your Majesty for not being a part of it!" Birbal mimicked a bow. Akbar looked away to hide, in spite of himself, his amusement. "Your Majesty," Birbal called as he followed the Emperor, "The Maharana could be hiding in the mountains…" Birbal quickly said in order to redeem himself. Akbar turned to face his interlocutor and with great patience repeated,

"In the mountains… Perhaps you are not as stupid as you seem. Now, show me I am not mistaken… because if you don't tell me more precisely where about I will send you speeding into those Aravalli hills, from whence you will never emerge…" Akbar's eyes widened as he thrust down his throat some wine from the goblet. "No one has ever returned from the Aravalli hills except that Pratap- the Bhils will boil you in a pot and eat you up!"

"Gogunda! Your Majesty. The Fortress of Gogunda…"

"Fortress, you call that a Fortress!!! It's made of cow dung and straw…"

"Like most fortresses, Sire. Intelligence has it," Birbal quickly added before Akbar would cut him off, "that the Maharana has reinforced the boundry walls of all his mountain fortresses…"

"Stop calling him Maharana... there is no king of kings- I am the Emperor!"

Akbar walked towards the centre of the court as he saw Sakta appear. "Ah," the Emperor mouthed, "just the person who can be of greater enlightment than these Navratnas I am surrounded with," and then in a louder tone, so as to be heard by all remarked, "The Sisodian's enstranged brother is more likely than any to guide me out of this wilderness." He swallowed the rest of the wine.

"Sire, whatever you command," Sakta said approaching and making some kind of attempt of bowing as low as he could, but not with great conviction, almost stumbling, which made little difference, as for the same reason, the Emperor was not too steady on his feet either.

"Where could that brother of yours be hiding in Mewar?" Akbar asked.

"Brother? Sire, I have no brother in Mewar." Sakta stood upright while Akbar motioned his servant to fill up a goblet for Sakta then signalled his General to join him. "I don't think Sakta Ji is in a state of clear mindedness," Akbar said in quiet tones. "However, Kunwar Man Singh, rather than occupy yourself in matters that are not within your range of comprehension like Christianity, I am going to entrust you with a special mission." Man Singh of Amber bowed in acceptance. "That half-relation of yours..." Akbar paused, "was not the late Maharana's sister, your grandfather's wife?"

"Great grandfather, my Liege," Man Singh corrected. Akbar looked puzzled. "Yes, Sire, because my grandfather's daughter, is here at the Imperial court as your wife..."

"Ah, my first wife, indeed," Akbar interrupted, "being a Raja's daughter made up for other blemishes..."

"Your wife, my Liege," Man Singh continued, "has no mother related to Pratap- it was my great grandfather that married Pratap's aunt." Akbar smiled wryly at himself at the way his General was able to sweep the lack of niceties of life under the carpet.

"As, I was saying," Akbar began again with his tone of confidentiality, "That half-relation of yours who has the audacity to rule over Mewar, without the least regard that I am the Emperor of India must be brought to bend a knee to my Royal person." Akbar looked earnestly at Man Singh... "you are well aware I will not accept failure..." Akbar paused. "The other five emissary, including your own father, the Raja, have all ended down the drain, and now it seems that half-figure of a man- because the other half is a savage- has gone into hiding again, Gogunda, some say."

"I could join him in Gogunda," the General offered.

"What! And if they set about you, how are you going to save your butt...?

"Sire, I am a Hindu, a Rajput, like them, flesh of their flesh... there is a code..."

"And you suppose those Barbarians will respect the code? How do you think you will return? There is no way out from Gogunda- at least not for us city folks."

Akbar paused thoughtfully, "As soon as I have news Pratap has repaired to Udaipur you will set about your mission." Akbar turned around restlessly. "I've offered that Sisodian gold, women, lands, armies, cannons, elephants... anything! So as to have his knee bend before my throne... one knee... that's all I ask..." Akbar flung back the wine in his goblet- "he can keep his temples, his gods, his rituals, his jahurs... and even though I see it not with a good eye, he can burn how many wives he wants on his funeral pyre... in exchange for just one knee..." Akbar looked away and whispered as if to himself... "and a virgin or two..."

CHAPTER SIXTEEN

An Incommodious Guest

Amar discusses with his father, Pratap, General Man Singh's mission; a dinner is prepared in honour of Man Singh but ends in a war council in Gogunda

A group of horsemen with the Imperial ensign were gallopping away from the Moti Magri dwellings of the new Mewar Capital in Udaipur when Patrap's trusted Treasurer and General, rode into the courtyard. Kunwar Amar, Patrap's Crown Prince, greeted him, "You arrive too late honourable Bhama Shah," the Prince said, "but there is no new tidings to enfold, another of Akbar's emissary with the same tale as told on previous occasions."

"Indeed Sire, but did I not perceive a distinguished General just passing by?"

"If by distinguished, you refer to that, as my father calls him, infidel Man Singh of Amber, then yes." Amar rubbed his chin. "Do me the service," he said turning to the Prime Minister, "accompany me to Gogunda and persuade the Maharana to return to his rightful capital..."

"With pleasure, my Liege," then astutely, Bhama Shah enquired, "I perceive you distance yourself from your father on the matter of facing the General?"

"The tactics of accommodation were never a priority in my father's resolutions. Diplomacy is an art my grandfather, has transmitted to my own self."

"Indeed, Maharana Udai favoured a living Ruler to a dead hero."

"You are not of that opinion, my honourable Sardar?" Amar paused, "As I well recall being informed it was you who invited my father to repair to the safety of Gogunda just before Akbar took Chittor..."

"It was no invitation, my Liege. Your father would have none of it- he insisted on staying and be killed- Stronger methods had to be employed." Bhama Shah rubbed his beard thoughtfully, "I believe the Sardars offered him the choice of Gogunda or a dungeon cell in Chittor."

"That's my father all right,"Amar smiled, "and if truth has it, he has worsened since we lost Chittor."

"He will not rest until he has regained it," Bhama Shah shook his head.

"You too, see the unlikely chance of regaining Chittor from Akbar by force, do you not my brave Bhama Shah?"

"Indeed, Sire. I see it so. Akbar has strange contraptions from the Portuguese- balls of fire that can shoot into unknown distances. "

"Then we must haste to Gogunda and persuade my noble father to seek other means of regaining Chittor."

"We have no gold my Lord. What was entrusted to me before the Emperor attacked Chittor is so depleted that even the Maharana no longer keeps court at Gogunda..."

"Do not be impressed that my father has chosen the life style of a near savage- that is not due to poverty but a natural state he feels totally comfortable with."

"I see Sire you cherish to make much sport of the Maharana's condition."

They walked along the courtyard towards the stables. Pratap's white Marwari stallion, Chetak, was awaiting proudly for his master's touch. "Negotiations, we must persuade the Maharana to negotiate." Amar insisted.

"With whom, my Lord, the General?"

"Yes Bhama Shah, the Emperor's emissary, Kunwar Man Singh of Amber."

"Pardon, my Lord, but the Maharana will not find it feasible to negotiate with one so below his own station... The General is only a Prince, a Kunwar, son of a Raja. Whereas your noble father is the Maharana, the King of Kings... A title which you aspire to, my Lord."

"Precisely so. And I intend not only to remain alive so as to have it bestowed upon me but also to possess the kingdom that goes with it."

"I see your meaning, Sire. If we do not give heed to Akbar's requests peacefully, Akbar will take them forcefully- and we shall all be dead and the tale will not be told."

"Perfectly so, Bhama Shah. Let's away. Gogunda awaits."

The bare-chested Bhils were in attendance as the two Nobles and their retinue rode into the courtyard of Gogunda. The sun was beginning to pierce through the bright, motionless blue sky, unto the dome of the Palace. Amar strode forth into the main hall glad of the coolness of the thick stone sheltering walls, which having retreated from the external light, made him feel as if he had suddenly plunged into darkness. He could see an undistinguishable figure coming towards him slowly. "My noble father," Amar said placing his hands together and bowing in the presence of the Maharana who had neared sufficiently for Amar's recognition, sword in hand and bow across the shoulder. "Hunting?" Amar enquired, "or is that your permanent state, father?" Pratap laughed roughly.

"Ah," he said loudly, "you find it in your genius to make fun of your father, I see." Amar smiled.

"Sometimes I look upon the figure of the Maharana with great difficulty..." Amar looked away uncomfortably from the lion skin clad Maharana.

"Does the sight cause my gracious son such distress?"

"Indeed father, such a sight as yours, grovelling in the dirt and nourishing your royal self on wild berries perturbs my conscience."

"And why should that be so? Have you not mettle enough to face the arrows and injuriousness of life?"

"My noble father needs at times be reminded that he is the Maharana of a kingdom."

"Which he would forfeit to that Mughal Emperor whose ambition in conquering the whole of our sacred land knows no restraint were I for a moment not prevent him from setting a foot inside this boundary; and that my dear son, entails continuously playing hide and seek with my opponent." Pratap placed his sword inside the sheath. "Hence it is my face is muddy and my knees rugged," he flicked the folds of the Prince's cloak, disdainfully with his forefinger, "and wear the skin of a lion instead of such genteel silks and satins as my son prefers to don."

"These cloths are but the stuff worthy of the noble rank that as your Crown Prince I hold, Sire."

"You need no fancy clothing to be my Crown Prince, your father the Maharana is but the Keeper of Mewar, only a Custodian... unlike the cumbersome pomp of the Mughal Emperor who struts around like some cockrel on show...." Pratap rubbed his beard thoughtfully; "Pray, what brings you with so much haste with my well loved, Treasurer to my presence? Not another emissary or... I should it is so?"

"You say right Father. And this time the General himself..." Pratap thundered with laughter;

"You appear in vein of gaming when you determine to attribute such importance to that speck of human mould that stains Mewar's soil... The General himself indeed..." Pratap mocked. "Is the Emperor not content with the message delivered to him by his last emissary? Or was he not happy to hear that 'Although the Maharana was of an exquisite graciousness, he reserved himself the right to say he wanted to keep his own knees quite upright and straight.'" Pratap said quoting himself upon the visit of the last Ambassador from the Imperial court. "And now that the spring enchants the air Akbar dares to defile it by sending General Man Singh himself? A mere Prince, son of a traitor, the Maharaja of Amber[39] who has given his sister in marriage to that infidel Akbar and dared defy Hindu, Rajput blood!"

"Father," Amar began, "General Man Singh has requested a dinner be called to negotiate an alliance with the Emperor."

"Ha!" the Maharana burst out, "rather than a reconciliation, Akbar is seeking to force me out into the open and cast me into irons or sever my own head from my body with this my own sword." Pratap pulled out his sword from his side and flashed it into the air. "My surrender, that is what the Emperor seeks and he will stoop at nothing less." Pratap walked pensively as he flashed the sword once more into space. "A dinner? The General seeks a dinner? Then he shall have one. Come!" Pratap beckoned with his sword let us repair to Udaipur and prepare the most magnificent meal the court of Mewar has seen for long on that splendid Lake Udaisagar, of my own Father's making;" he added with a touch of pride, then turning stopped and warned, "After which we will prepare a war council at the fortress in Gogunda."

Hence, in answer to his guest's auto invitation, Pratap set up an immense feast on the magnificent lake which perfectly reflected in its waters the immense red Indian twilight of the sky. But it was here, precisely at this feast as Pratap had foreseen, the events which led to the Battle of Gogunda, otherwise known as the Battle of Haldighati, had root. The General had aimed at sitting at the banquet next to the Maharana and eat out of the same plate, but for the Maharana this action was to him repugnant and so as not to create conflict decided to abstain from attending with the excuse of being indisposed due to a bad indigestion and sent his son, heir to the throne, Crown Prince Amar.

---

39 Now Jaipur

Informed of this, through a messenger the General told the Maharana that he had a certain powder that would put instant remedy to the Maharana's lack of well being. Pratap replied with gracious courtesy that he would be unable to sit next to a Rajput whose aunt is the mother of the heir to the throne of the Mughal Emperor and even less eat with such a one. The General withdrew instantly threatening that he would return and if he then did not induce the Maharana to bend not only one but both knees, his name was not Man Singh, to which the Maharana's spokesman reminded the General not to forget to bring his uncle (Akbar) with him.

All this being thus reported to the Emperor in great detail but Akbar, having problems elsewhere to attend to, decided to entrust his revenge at a time in the future when he could best dedicate himself with all his might to the utter ruin of Pratap and savour such delights in a more leisurely manner.

CHAPTER SEVENTEEN

THE BATTLE OF HALDIGHATI

June 18th 1576

Two years passed when in the spring of 1576 Akbar decides that the time had come to get Pratap to bend not one but both his knees. He formed a strong army of which naturally he placed General Man Singh at the head. Aware of the hatred that flowed between the General and the Maharana, Akbar was convinced that his choice of leadership would serve as bait for the not-to-be-found Pratap to come out from the depths of the rocks of the Aravalli. Pratap would never have given up the chance to challenge Man Singh in battle, and once out in the open, Pratap would be completely overwhelmed by the seven or more thousand Imperial cavalry against the less than three thousand Rajputs of Pratap's army. With this strategy, Pratap's defeat was assured.

On 3rd May 1576, Man Singh of Amber left Ajmer with an army of five thousand men with orders from Akbar to destroy Mewar. On the way, he stopped at the fortress of Mandal Garh to be joined by other warriors from the Imperial army, who were not in the least Mughals but Hindus and Rajputs of the same faith and descent of the Maharana. They had been conquered in the past and defeated by Akbar having no other choice but to succumb to the Emperor. This was also another reason for having chosen Man Singh as Leader of the army, as most of the soldiers forming the military were Rajputs, they would have fought with a little less misgivings as they were not so enthusiastic, so as not to say, found it repulsive, when in battle with their fellow Rajputs on the other side. However, with Man Singh as their General, they would find more desire to remain faithful to their Mughal but nevertheless Rajput Commander.

One has to say that at the time of these events, the outcome of a battle often depended on the mood of the warriors themselves. This is why the role of the legendary Bhills who are renowned for their valiant defence of Pratap has to be highlighted. Being one who did not take kindly to the luxurious life at court, but also through necessity, Pratap had, even from infancy embraced the Spartan life of those forbidding hills, he knew how to survive and feed himself among the barren rocks and thorny bushes of the Aravalli, and more, he knew one by one the multitude of inhabitants of this desolate, barren land, namely the Bhills who were in effect the true natives of India whose origins are traceable even as far back as fifteen hundred years before Christ and beyond. It was indeed, one of these natives of the Aravalli forest that consecrated the first Ruler of Mewar, Guhil, a thousand years beforehand in 569 A.D. as was shown at the beginning of this narrative. Therefore these Bhills, at this crucial moment, when the Mewar Ruler had so great need of them rallied around he, whom they considered their Lord, with indestructible fidelity. It was precisely this that Akbar feared, the strong bond that kept the Bhills united to the Maharana, because no one better than they were more acquainted with those 600 kilometres of rocks that went beyond one thousand metres in height. To plan an ambush for the Imperial soldiers at any moment, in any place, for the Bhils would simply be child's play.

Therefore it was the Bhils who guarded their Royal Lord, kept under control every kind of movement that the Imperial army would take and when they saw the troops gathering at Mandalgarh, Pratap marched down from his fortress in Kumbalgarh and reunited all his nobles and warriors at the fortress of Gogunda below, which as we may well remember is placed right in the middle of those 600 kilometres of the daunting rocks of the Aravalli hills ready in waiting to attack Mandalgarh immediately. The astuteness of General Man Singh of bringing Pratap down unto the plain, was about to work. It were due his elders to put a restraint on pratap's desire for immediate combat who pointed out to him the folly of this manoeuvre. On the plain they would be quite overcome by the Mughal army which overcame in numbers that of the Maharana's by twice the amount. Hence, although the desire to fight Man Singh was immense, Pratap realized that his nobles were right and the General would have to come to the Maharana not vice-versa. Pratap also considered that such a battle would only end in a lot of needless loss of Rajput blood, both on their side and that of the enemy without in the least damaging Akbar since as Akbar himself proclaimed when asked how a Rajput from the Imperial army could be distinguished and therefore saved from that of a Rajput of the Maharana: Akbar himself noted that it made no difference to him- as the slaughter of a Rajput from whichever side he came from was always a gain for Islam.[40]

After two hours that the sun had risen above the horizon of those North-Western hills, on that 18th June 1576, the faithful Bhils spotted three columns of vast numbers of warriors rise from the Mughal camp positioned on the Khamnor plain below and heading in the direction of the Aravalli mountain chain. The central column led by the General was heading towards the mouth opening of the extremely narrow path known as, the Haldighati Pass, which would lead to the Fortress of Gogunda, while both sides of this trail were swallowed up by the wild foliage of the forest without respite of escape. The General was intent in entering this formidable passage so as to proceed to Gogunda where he was certain Pratap was hiding. However Pratap was not at the fortress but right there at the neck of the Haldighati passage, protected by the thick foliage, waiting for his adversary to arrive.

The battle scene that followed was reported by the same war correspondent from the Imperial court as mentioned previously, Al Badayuni, therefore not reported from the advantage point of view of the Mewar troops. It is precisely from this correspondent that we learn the Imperial troops, completely stunned by the vigorous impact with the Maharana warriors, upon estranged ground, full of thorns and rocks, not able to defend themselves had to abandon the fight and flee back to the safety of the plain.

The column of warriors headed by the Maharana sprang out from the mouth of the Haldighati Pass with such force that it swept away all the Imperial forces on the threshold of entering the Pass. Pratap continued to ride on his beloved white stallion, Chetak, in search of General Man Singh destroying anyone who attempted to bar his way. While the Imperial soldiers were scattering everywhere, the command was given to bring forth the war elephants-in-waiting on the Imperial side. But in killing the rider of such, being left without guide the war elephants being armed with a special sword in their trunk that tore to pieces whatever came within reach, trampled and devastated whatever stood before them, creating panic and destruction all around.

---

40 This particolar quote was noted by the Imperial war correspondent Al Badayuni

Suddenly a shrill war cry rising from a Mewar warrior[41] pierced the air, he had sighted General Man Singh himself at the helm of an Imperial war elephant. Standing up on his stirrups, knowing he would have no chance of survival, the valiant Rajput threw his spear directly at the General who, cleverly avoiding the thrust the lance flew by, leaving him completely harmless while the Mughal attendants besieged, the sword in hand faithful Rajput. The Maharana hearing the warning from his devoted Rajput dashed with fury to the spot, cutting down all who came between him and his so much hated adversary. Chetak, Pratap's white stallion lifted its hoofs against the vast clump of the elephant, as Pratap hurled a fierce blow at the howda[42] where General Man Singh was sitting. Stunned, shocked and confused by the blow, Man Singh nevertheless managed to disappear behind the howda, and for a brief moment Pratap savoured the glory of having annihilated his adversary.

Immediately Pratap was surrounded by Imperial warriors and although he managed to cause a massacre, it was a critical moment especially as unaware to Pratap the elephant's war-sword had inflicted a horrific slash across Chetak's hind legs. At a certain point as Pratap was slaughtering one of the Imperial commanders, another Mughal chief lifted his sabre to sever the Maharana's head when Pratap suddenly hearing a wild cry of warning turned immediately, with a backhand struck the sabre of his would be executioner and made it fly a far distance. The Maharana looked around him furtively to discover from whom the cry came and noted it was his estranged brother Sakta who had defected to Akbar's court after many a brawl with Pratap in youth. Blood is thicker than water, Pratap thought, and alongside his brother and the Mewar warriors, continued to strike down the Imperial forces preventing them to advance into the Haldighati Pass. Arrows were whistling through the air, the hammering of sabres on the rocks thundered, and everywhere blood was flowing. Those of the Imperial army who did not flee where trapped in the Pass under the blows of the Mewar warrior sabres.

At one point a commotion rising from the Imperial forces could be heard. The news spread quicker than blazing fire that Akbar, the Emperor himself had arrived. Instinctively Patrap felt the urge to throw himself into a direct battle confrontation, but then he thought better and heeded the advice of his warriors. If Akbar had arrived, then he certainly would have brought with him an army more immense than the one his nephew,

---

41   Dodiya Bheem of Sardargarh
42   The driver's seat in the shape of a chest placed on the back of an elephant

General Man Singh had taken; and without doubt his army would consist of authentic Mughal warriors, without a trace of Rajput blood in them to stave off their appetite for slaughter. Therefore, Pratap, thinking erroneously to have annihilated General Man Singh and having made his presence felt on the battlefield, forcing the major part of the Imperial troops to withdraw, he was satisfied; hence ordering the retreat of his troops even though this meant an admission of defeat.

Fate would have it that two of Pratap's greatest commanders were called that same name the General of the Mughal army bore, with the difference that they were both from the Jhala House and therefore direct ancestors of the Rulers of Gogunda Palace. The first, Raja Man Singh of Delwara with whom Pratap's father, Udai had often gone hunting and who had tested the then young heir to Delwara with the capture of a bull. Jhala Man Singh had several offsprings but only the two heirs have been recorded in annals, one who was to inherit Delwara and the other, Shatrushal was to inherit Gogunda which was gifted to their father Jhala Man Singh for services rendered to the Court of Mewar.

The second Raja Man Sing was a cousin from Bari Sadri, also in Mewar and was known as Raja Bida. When Pratap gave the order to retreat these two commanders remained on the battle field so as to stave off the Mughal warriors from following the Maharana into the Haldighati Pass, the only means of reaching the Fortress of Gogunda. Raja Bida took up the Mewar insignia, the golden rays of a yellow gold sun on a bright red background and for certain, when Pratap turned, this flag flying above a field of blood was the last image he saw knowing that it would only be a matter of moments before it would fall and be covered in the blood of the valiant Rajput that had upheld it. And so it was. The two Jhala cousins, both named Man Singh as the Mughal Genral who had slaughtered them, were recorded on the list of those who fell for Mewar. However, it was through their resistance that the Maharana of Mewar, their much loved Ruler escaped from being captured and was able to flee among those imperious rocks that had always shielded him. Unfortunately it did not prevent the Imperial forces to enter the Haldighati Pass and slaughter those few servants who had remained behind at the Fortress of Gogunda.

During the fighting, while all of the Imperial troops were engaged in defeating and capturing Pratap around the vicinity of the Haldighati Pass, hordes of Bhils, the renown natives of the Aravalli hills faithful to the Maharana, slid with agility into where the Mughals had placed their supplies and what they could not carry back they destroyed on the spot.

Hence the seven thousand strong army of the Emperor, without food and supplies was rendered quite useless. For a while, Pratap hid in the Aravalli hills which no Mughal could approach and then retreated to the forbidding fortress of Kumbhalgarh with the bitterness of not having overcome his most despised Rival, and the meagre consolation that the inconclusive Battle of Haldighati was scripted for others to perceive as:

> *"No defeat more glorious.*
> *No victory less noble."*

PART TWO

Part Two of the history is based on an account compiled by the inhabitants of the area in the local Mewari dialect. The work was commissioned by Sajjan Singh Mewar 1874-1884 who requested the local people of Gogunda to set down their history which was written in the form of poetry by an Audhichya Brahmin

CHAPTER EIGHTEEN

Pratap flees to the wilderness of Chavan; Gogunda is taken away from the Delwara heirs; Shatrushal abandons Mewar and returns; the battle at Diwar 1582; the distress and death of Pratap

Up to this point the fortress of Gogunda was in the custody of the Maharana and used as an extension of the throne of Mewar but after the defeat at Haldighati it was occupied by the Imperial forces and therefore out of the Maharana's control. The Maharana himself hides within the hills of the Aravalli and with the help of his ever faithful Bhils carries out successful guerrilla attacks which defeats three of Akbar's campaigns. But in the Spring of 1577 the Emperor returns with might and force- this time the Maharana lost to Akbar. Completely abated, Pratap retreats to the mighty walls of Khumbalgarh where it would be a problem even for Akbar to penetrate. But Akbar had other plans, he poisons the water of the main well by infesting it with insects and in so doing forcing Pratap on the move, this time to Chavand where Pratap could be protected by the Bhils who inhabited the vast area of wilderness which made up Chavand.

For almost three years Pratap survives on wild berries and whatever meagre substance the wilderness of Chavand would yield. In the meantime he was gathering whatever remained of his Rajput warriors about him, this included Kalyan, Jhala Man Singh's Crown Prince, who after the death of his father at the battle of Haldighati inherits Delwara, even though, having to forgo the coronation ceremonies since most of the estates of the Maharana's Rajputs were in the hands of the Mughal Emperor nor were there any funds so as to perform them. Nevertheless the tax due to the Maharana in order for a ruler to take up office, especially in these drastic circumstances of the Mewar throne, could not be overlooked. This also applied to Gogunda Palace which had been promised to Jhala Man Singh for his services at the Battle of Haldighati. However Jhala Man's second son and Kalyan's brother, Shatrushal, had no funds to give to the Maharana and hence Pratap "gifted" Gogunda, in other words gave it to him who paid a good deal to gain the Raja's title which happened to have been a certain Manmandas Rathore Rajput of Badnore.

This of course did not much please Shatrushal who thought best to leave the Maharana's services and go where he was wanted instead, or so he thinks; namely to Jodphur where he has family ties, his aunt had married the previous Ruler of Jodhpur, Rao Maladeo. There, Shatrushal is given an estate. Meanwhile back at Chavand some rulers and Pratap's Crown Prince Amar plea on behalf of Shatrushal that Gogunda should not be given to a stranger. It seemed that Kalyan too was temporarily usurped of Delwara for Manmandas went directly to Delwara supported by a retinue of five nobles and took up office there. So it was that Kalyan left Delwara and went to Gujarat where he was joined by other nobles who requested Kalyan to go and get Shatrushal so their power be strengthened by their union- and besides the Maharana needed money, yes, but he also needed first and above all, valiant Rajputs in his kingdom so as to regain the lands the Emperor had conquered.

Meanwhile having received news from Mewar, Shatrushal informs the Raja of Jodhpur that the Mughal forces were moving to Udaipur, meaning of course that the Marahana was in danger of being suppressed which meant the least Jodhpur could do, being a Rajput Princely State, was join forces with the Maharana to stave off the Emperor. But since a great number of the Ruler's sisters and even a daughter of his had married Akbar, the ground was well prepared for a heated discussion between the two Chieftains, which indeed followed with the consequence that Shatrushal went off in a huff towards Godwar to meet his brother Kalyan on the border of Mewar and Marwar now known as Jodhpur. There, Kalyan explained that Pratap was in great difficulty, surviving only on wild berries, roaming the wilderness and in great need of Shatrushal. But Shatrushal was no longer disposed to be at the service of the Marahana, probably because he had no funds to pay for occupying the seat of Gogunda as Raja and was not prepared to go back without an estate to go to. However Kalyan explained that in the past both of them had enjoyed the gifts the Maharana had showered upon them, had eaten of his food and many privileges, and now in difficult days it was their duty to fight in the defence of their Maharana. This was the reason, Kalyan emphasized that the Maharana had sent for the return of Shatrushal from Jodhpur, to fight against the Emperor and nothing else- at which point be it because the

Ruler of Jodhpur was too close in parental relationship to the Emperor for comfort, or be it that his Hindu Rajput blood was making claims on his conscience, Shatrushal accepts.

The Ruler of Deogarh, Shatrushal himself and his brothers including Kalyan with an infantry of 400 soldiers, and a calvary of 200 horses march towards Kumbhalgarh which the Mughals had captured by totally infesting the waters with insects. The three Chieftains advanced steadily to where the enemy was camping and was placing a great pressure on the Mewar Army. When the conflict broke out, the three Rajputs fought fiercely forcing the Mughal army to retreat two miles. The Lord of Deogarh was killed and so was another much loved brother of Shatrusal. Mewar had lost one thousand and five hundred soldiers but neither was the Mughal army spared, two thousand died. Kalyan and Shatrusal fought bravely but with severe consequences for Shatrushal.

These and the following description of the events that occurred are taken from the Khyat which is a poem written in Mewari, a language now extinct; retaining the simplicity of the original interpretation also using the same titles given for rulers. As one reads the delicacy and diplomacy in which these events are described it comes to mind if the ferociousness with which Akbar inflected upon Mewar was only directed towards the Maharana and not to others, however, we know this is not so as in the previous sack of Chittor, he well and truly swept away all that even partially smelt of Hindu blood. Nevertheless, the author of the Khyat sees the treatment Muslims served upon their royal captives as full of dignity befitting to the noble status of their confined.

Shatrusal, received twenty-nine injuries, unable to be moved, he and his brother took shelter in a temple dedicated to Lord Shiva which was near by. Skilfully Kalyan hid Shatrushal so carefully that he was able to stave off the enemy so no one could go near the wounded body of Shatrusal. However, this could not last for long, eventually the enemy found Kalyan and the Bashah[43] ordered his soldiers to bring Kalyan to him. A Nawab[44] was sent for Kalyan, which meant he was now a prisoner of Akbar. As Kalyan had no arms or means of defending himself, he surrendered inside the temple. This would appear like a modern day political refugee status. Kalyan requested the Nawab to allow his men to take care of his wounded brother.

---

43 Another title used for Akbar
44 Title of Muslim Ruler or Prince

The Nawab promised Kalyan to take care of his brother as well as Kalyan's reputation as a soldier and that he would be treated as a royal prince. Kalyan came out of the temple and was mounted with the Nawab on the same elephant. Meanwhile Kalyan's turban fell off. The Nawab exchanged his turban with Kalyan's turban and called him brother. The exchange of turbans between a Muslim and Hindu occurs on other occasions and is the a sign of extreme cordiality and friendship between two strangers or had been enemies. Badshah was very pleased to see him and took him to Delhi, not that Kalyan had any choice as the Khayt seems to suggest by the use of such terminology.

But back to Shatrushal's recovery at the hands of the Muslims. Once recovered both brothers were free to leave. Why this was so no one has made the point of noting it, but it is doubtful a ransom was paid since no one had the indication of a rupee anywhere in the kingdom of Mewar. At which point Kalyan returns to Pratap and asks that Shatrushal be given Gogunda again. Pratap said he could not since he had gifted it to the Rathore and until this Rathore lived, Gogunda could not be regained.

In spite of the fact that Pratap did not concede Gogunda Palace to Shatrushal, the would be Raja of Gogunda remained to fight for the Maharana and being thus fully occupied in war, it was no great significance to him whether or not he could take up his throne at Gogunda, after all Akbar was sweeping in and out continuously with all his retinue, occupying the Raja's Palace more often than the rightful resident, Manmandas of Badnore was. In all fairness to Pratap, apart from the tax matter, the Maharana was in debt to the Royal family of Badnore whose rulers in turn had given their lives to fight for the Maharana, at the sack of Chittor and at Haldighati, but in no less measure had Shatrushal's father and his father before him given their lives in saving that of their Maharana in both the same battles. However not all battles were lost. He was encouraged by the gesture that every Rajput Chieftain in Mewar and beyond, who had not been conquered by the Imperial forces gathered around him, but what brought the greatest joy to Pratap was to see his son, Crown Prince Armar, whom Pratap feared to be too much a lover of court life, take on the command of the battle which brought a decisive victory in favour of Mewar at the strategic town of Diwer, previously conquered by the Imperial forces in an attempt to spread their power southwards.

After this battle at Diwar in 1582, Amar continued his command of the Mewar warriors under whom, Shatrushal had no regrets in serving, in spite that Amar's enthusiasm for battle on one occasion got the better of him. In one of the nearby villages where the Mughal Commander Khan Khana had camped, Prince Amar captured all the wives of the Commander and with great pride and joy presented them to his father, the Maharana. Pratap was aghast, he reminded Amar in no uncertain terms that he was a Rajput and ordered his Crown Prince to return the said ladies back to their rightful owner, the defeated Mughal Commander, without touching a hair on their head. A grateful Khan Khana was delighted to have his ladies back and became a life-long friend and admirer of the Rajput Prince, but above all, that of his father, the Maharana.

Even though Pratap regained Kumbhalgarh, Udaipur and most of his lands excluding of course, what he had always endeavoured to recapture- Chittorgarh- he nevertheless continued to live in the wilderness of Chavand and demanded that his subjects too followed him there thus emptying completely the new capital that his father, Maharana Udai had built, namely Udaipur. He was beleaguered by the thought that there were no provisions to feed his family and weighed down by the worry that his family, wives, sons would be captured for he was certain, the Mughals would not have the chivalry of a Rajput that he, the Maharana himself showed when Amar captured the wives of the Mughal Commander Khan Khana. At times he had to resort to the Bhils carrying the women and children in wicker baskets and hiding them in the Zawar mines.

He was also fraught by the loss of so many of his lifelong friends and valiant Rajput Chieftains who had without a second thought sacrificed their lives, so that he, their Maharana could live. But to Pratap this life, without regaining his much loved Chittorgarh, meant nothing to him and at the threshold of poverty, starvation for himself, his family, his subjects and the remembrance of the dead warrior Rajputs on the battlefield, he dammed the name of sovereignty. With immense regret, the Maharana decided to send a message to Akbar for a "mitigation of his hardships." On contemplating his distressed circumstances, Pratap would try with all the energy remaining to validate this pitiful state with the saying "For this the Rajput was born."

Some say the Maharana left Mewar and was on his way to the Indus Valley when he was unexpectedly presented with the revenue from the kingdom that his Treasurer Bhama Shah had taken into safety on the vigil of the Battle of Haldighati but much was also added by the Treasurer himself from his own personal resources. Though it was also the fact that every Rajput considered Pratap as their only hope of regaining their freedom from Mughal domain that prevented Pratap from surrendering to Akbar and for the following ten years, before his death in 1597 at the relative early age of 56, took up the defence of his Kingdom once more. However, be it that Akbar, who secretly admired his Rajput opponent, or be it that his attention was taken up in expanding the Mughal Empire Northwest in Punjab, the Emperor for the rest of Pratap's life, relented his aggression on Mewar.

Although Armar had proved himself a valiant warrior, Pratap had never overcome his misgivings about his heir. The Maharana feared that Amar loved the life of ease and would abandon the Spartan hills of Gogunda for the comforts that the life at court in Udaipur could offer. Therefore as Pratap lay dying in Chavand, he made Amar promise never to succumb to Mughal power or be lured to the life of ease that Udaipur could offer but be always vigilant and never sacrifice Mewar to foreign power.

CHAPTER NINETEEN

Amar invites the people to leave Chavand and return to Udaipur which he makes his capital; Akbar's successor, Jahangir, renews Mughal aggression on Mewar; Gogunda is taken by Jahangir; there are disputes among Gogunda's Jhala heirs; Amar's agreement of compromise with the Emperor; Amar's Crown Prince Karen at the Imperial court and his friendship with the Emperor's son, Khurram; Gogunda taken over by Rathores of Idar; dispute between Gogunda's heirs; Emperor Aurangzeb dethrones Raja of Jodhpur; Raj I Mewar breaks 1615 Treaty and restores Chittor; Aurangzeb attacks Udaipur and Raj I is made homeless;1736 Maratha Rao captures Udaipur; end of the Mughal Empire

With the death of his father, and Akbar seemingly to have lost interest in conquering Mewar at all costs, Amar set himself to better the condition of his people and invited them all to abandon the wilderness of Chavant and return to Udaipur which he once again made the capital. Thus, Pratap's fears about his son proved in part a reality and Amar exchanged the austere life of the Gogunda hills for the court life of Udaipur. Amar then set himself to improve the conditions of his war-torn subjects by reassessing land holdings, distributing fiefs and establishing a new system of ranking for the nobility. It is at this point that the title of Raja for the ruler of Gogunda was now finally established during this particular period of reassessment but the throne remained empty yet again since after the death of Akbar in 1605, the new Ruler Emperor Jahangir forgets whatever private pact of peace had been made between his father and Pratap, and the aggression on Mewar begins as fierce as ever before.

During the relative period of peace Akbar conceded to Mewar for the period of his last years on this earth, Shatrushal had well and truly established his family, a rather unusual one for the times, nevertheless it seems, because Shatrushal was absent most of the time being engaged in warfare, and the ladies, his wives, of which there were two for certain had the upper hand in the household and educated the children the way they saw fit, which may not often be the best way by any means. Shatrushal's first born, and heir to Gogunda Palace Nathu, conceived from his first wife who was very much an overprotective mother made sure Nathu, in spite of being Crown Prince Raja would never be out of her sight and in the hands of those that were to make of him a Ruler. Hence she refused to send him to the Sarders who wanted to train him as a heir of a Raja saying her son Nathu would enjoy the milk and rice in the forest where he would take pleasure in hunting the deer in safety. His brother Kanah, from a lesser wife, for indeed there were ranks in wives too, had a much easier and by far more exciting time, ending up much less petulant and independent, than Nathu.

Meanwhile, their father Shatrushal, unaware of such goings-on fought yet another brilliant battle against one of a succession of Generals, Abdulla Khan in 1609, sent by Jahangir to conquer Mewar. Shatrushal was seriously wounded but not without having slaughtered the Mughal Commander first. However, shortly afterwards the Emperor swept with force across Mewar capturing Gogunda, forcing Amar to recuperate his forces in the Aravalli hills while Shatrushal falls in a brave attempt to attack the Imperial check-post at Ravalia with disastrous consequences for Mewar.

The death of Shatrushal too had its own particular consequences on the domestic side. One of his lesser wives was placed on the funeral pyre, and it must have been Kanah's mother since he, who at the time was only three years old, was made to live with his half-brother Nathu, while Shatrushal's first wife was spared so she could smother Nathu, their first born with loving care and attention, keep him from harm's way hunting deer in the forest, drinking milk and eating sweet berries from the wild trees! It was really of no great consequence that Amar, pleased with Shatrushal's faithfulness, returned the throne of Gogunda to Shatrushal's heir, whoever that may have been since it was not certain the mother would let go of her hold upon Nathu. However, to become the Raja of Gogunda Palace was of no great consequence anymore to anyone because there was no throne to give to whomsoever could claim it as by the year 1611 Jahangir swept over Mewar against Amar and took control of six main cities including Udaipur and Gogunda.

After seventeen battles, Amar's army was severely depleted and it was no comfort to him that he had fought a great deal many more battles than his father, the Kingdom's hero, Pratap, ever had. However, unlike his father whose courage knew no bounds, Amar knew when he was beaten and the futility in not admitting it. This notion came clearly to him when the Enperor's son, Prince Khurram encamped in Gogunda with a strong, vigorous army and would not be moved. There was nothing more to be done Amar's warriors, what remained of them, could nowhere near match the Imperial forces so he reluctantly set out a peace proposal and sent two ambassadors to present the document to the Prince. Khurram consulted his father who agreed on the peace terms set out by Amar himself.

Amar worded his proposal diligently knowing full well any agreement would have to include a Mewar royal presence at the Imperial court and armed support. Therefore in this proposal, Amar sought a compromise and stated that no Marahana would be present at a Mughal court but the Crown Prince would be sent instead; this was to respect his father's dying wish that no Maharana would bend a knee at the Imperial court. Another vital point which also reflected Pratap's strong views on the matter was that there would be no matrimonial alliance or Imperial title. And finally what was most dear to the defund Maharana was that Chittor would be regained, while conceding it would not be restored, (a point which will later cause conflict between Raj Singh 1 (1653-1680) and Aurangzeb). Of course it was to go without saying that the Maharana would provide one thousand horsemen when demanded. Thus in February 1615 this peace treaty was signed at Gogunda Palace. Prince Khurram and Amar became firm friends, it is said, which was to continue in Karan's reign after Amar's abdication in 1620 which he did so because of the remorse in having compromised with the Mughals.

It is unfortunate that Shatursal's heir of Gogunda was called Kanah and Shatrusal's brother was called Kalyan, because to complicate matters, Amar's heir of Mewar was called Karan. However, Karan, the future fifty-sixth Ruler to the throne of Mewar was the one who had the added dilemma of having a Muslim Prince as a close friend since due to Amar's peace treaty of 1614, Karan, as Crown Prince had to spend some time at the Mughal court and consequently became the inseparable friend of Khurram, the Emperor's heir, later to become Shah Jahan, remembered for having built the Taj Mahal, and in old age, deposed and imprisoned by his son- the fearful Aurangzeb. The Khyat, repeatedly, tells of an episode where the exchange of turbans occurs between Karan, the Crown Prince of Mewar and Khurram, the Mughal Crown Prince. A similar episode happened to Kalyan of Delwara, with the Nawab when he was taken prisoner in the temple. The exchange of turbans was a frequently practised custom to show honour and friendship.

During his reign, 1620-1628, Karan rebuilt much of his capital Udaipur, adding many rooms, courtyards and halls to the City Palace. He constructed Zenana Mahal which was a palace for the Queens on the south side of the Palace. His most renowned achievement was the construction of a pleasure palace on an island in Pichola Lake called Jag Mandir in 1622 but was terminated by his son Jagat I. It was in this palace that a year later, Karan gave refuge to his Mughal friend Prince Khurram who had rebelled against his father.

This friendship between Karan of Mewar and Khurram ensured that Karan's eight year reign was peaceful, which was not the case in Gogunda. In spite of a revised copy of a document showing that Maharana Karan of Mewar had gifted several villages to Kanah of Gogunda in 1619, Kanah, Shatrushal's son, was not able to take possession of the Palace as it was otherwise occupied by others, at this point in time, by the Rathores. As soon as the Mughals had vacated the Palace, Kanah of Gogunda had to defend his throne from the Rathores, due to a claim that the throne of Gogunda had, in the past, been gifted by Pratap to Mammandas Rathore. As it is claimed in the Khyat: "Idariya Rathore (the clan from Gujarat) was ruling over Gogunda at the time and had established a 'Thana' (a sort of military police station), with five hundred men at his service." In 1628, Kanah marched on Gogunda and drove away the Rathores and all of Idar's police were removed from the villages. In that dispute one hundred and fifty men were killed including a Dayiya (a noble Rajput) whose dagger was left in commemoration. Kanah, himself was also wounded, it is noted. However, once rid of the Rathore occupation, Kanah was still not able to reign on the throne of Gogunda. His older brother Nathu, hearing that Kanah had freed Gogunda, decided it was time to claim the throne for himself. Obviously he no longer enjoyed hunting the deer in the forest drinking milk and eating berries. But Kanah had already claimed the throne and Nathu was not made welcomed by anyone in Gogunda, so Nathu left Gogunda and set out for Delwara where his uncle Kalyan gave him a Madder (an estate) on lease, worth 15,000 Rupees, (calculated value as at present: $500.00. Gogunda was worth 24,000 Rupees, about $900.00). Nathu's position was considered an inferior one to that of his younger brother, but that was no one's fault but his own, he should have woken up earlier. But then he had a mother who kept sending him to sleep.

Hence is the reason why, although Amar of Mewar had restored Gogunda to Shatrusal's heir more than twenty years earlier, Kanah had not been able to take the throne of Gogunda until 1619. Initially, when his father died, Kanah was too young to claim the throne, and it was anyway occupied by the Rathore to whom it had been gifted. Then Gogunda was captured and occupied by the Mughals who returned it to the Rathores (the Mughals and the Rathores had marriage alliances). But Kanah, in typical Rajput style won what was rightly his through his own efforts in battle.

This explains why Kanah's reign is recorded to begin as late as 1619 even though the Khyat shows that he was crowned King in 1614 and that the Talwar Bandhai (sword ceremony of inauguration) was carried out a year later. Once having took possession of Gogunda, Kanah asked the Mewar ruler of the time, Jagat I, to formally gift Gogunda to him, thus establishing the ownership once and for all. The deeds show part of this took place in 1645, which may refer to other property since a copy of another paravana[45] dealing with Gogunda was also issued in 1619.

In 1628, Karan of Mewar dies after eight years rule and his successor is Jagat I, who in turn, dies in 1652. Jagat's successor Raj Singh I is crowned in 1653 while Kanah of Gogunda remains firmly on the throne enjoying a very long reign throughout these three successions in Mewar.

At about the age of forty-five, Kanah of Gogunda still had no son so it was planned to adopt Rajang from Godach as heir to Gogunda. But after setting his eyes on a suitable maid of royal blood and this time really trying his hardest, the adoption proved to be no longer necessary as a son was at last born, Jaswant. By the time Jaswant was a young man, Raj Singh I 1653-1680 had succeed his father Jagat to the throne of Mewar.

Raj Singh I of Mewar proved to be a wise and constructive ruler, not only did he reorganize the State but also constructed many new buildings in Mewar including the reinforcement of Chittor begun by his father Jagat, thus breaking the peace treaty signed by Amar at Gogunda in 1614. A much displeased Prince Khurram, now known as Shah Jahan, marched into Mewar but the Maharana gave him elephants and gifts which appeased the Emperor and the situation was carried no further until the Emperor's son, Aurangzeb (1658-1707), succeed to the Mughal throne and planned a massive attack against Mewar. But then of Aurangzed this was to be expected being a reckless, ruthless and impatient ruler. Not wanting to wait around for his turn to reign, if ever he got there, managed to rid himself of his five older siblings, deposed his father, locked him up in a prison cell that could overlook the Taj Mahal where Shah Jahan's

---

45 Legal document

precious wife had been buried, and took over the throne, crowning himself Emperor of the Mughal Empire.

No sooner was he in power, Aurangzeb decided he would dabble a little with being a Ruler and ordered the Raja of Jodhpur (Rathores of Marwar but also Rajputs) who had surrendered to the Mughals and married Mughal Princesses this being a requisite of surrender, to leave his kingdom and palace as this was to be taken over by whomever the Emperor willed to live there. Hence the Raja of Jodhpur, with what remained of the royal family, most of whom having been exterminated as the Raja needed a little persuasion to be moved, was ordered to go to Delhi where the Mughal capital was so an eye could be kept upon him, next best thing to house arrest it would seem.

On the way one of the queens gave birth to a son, Ajit. Fearing that Aurangzeb would kill the infant the Rathores took the child to Raj Singh of Mewar who not only gave him refuge but also a jagir, Kherwa which had been given to Sajja's[46] son Jait by the Rathores as a wedding present. This infuriated Aurangzeb who immediately attacked the capital and sacked Udaipur which meant that the Maharana, Raj Singh was quite homeless, thus escaping to the refuge of the Aravalli hills as all his fore-fathers had done before him. In order to prevent the Mughal forces from entering the Aravalli hills area, Raj Singh drew together all his forces and in particular that of Kanah of Gogunda and his son Jaswant.

During the aggression of Aurangzeb, which lasted a good half century, three rulers had succeed to the throne of Mewar, Raj I, Jai I and finally his son Amar II. In Gogunda the throne had also been succeeded three times, Kanah I, Jaswant I and Ram I. From what is possible to follow from the events in the historical records available, towards the end of Aurangzeb's Reign, Jaswant of Gogunda sent his son Ram, not only to defend Gogunda from the Mughals, which had become, as in the past, a strategic position of entrance and escape, but also from the Rathores who had established themselves in that area due to Raj's protection at the beginning of Aurangzeb's reign in 1658.

This is allegedly shown in a document (paravana) issued during the reign of Raj I of Mewar. The letter greeted the newly crowned Jaswant of Gogunda, wishing him happiness, then disclosed the secret news of the Army of Aurangzeb preparing to attack and ordered Jaswant to procure some arms, otherwise the Maharana of Mewar would show his grave

---

46 The brother of Ajja who bore the standard flag and saved the great Sanga, a century earlier

displeasure and Jaswant of Gogunda might be the victim of the Maharana's anger.

In 1684, when Aurangzeb had reigned sixteen years, as one of the most ruthless Mughal Rulers in history, a letter was sent, this time to the Crown Prince of Gogunda, Ram Singh, as the father Jaswant, was getting on in years and the young Prince who was not getting any younger either, needed some infantry exercise. In this letter Jai Singh of Mewar, Raj's son, appointed the Crown Prince of Gogunda to face the Nawab.

The Khyat never mentions the name of the Nawab, but the Mughal Ruler at the time was the said ferocious Aurangzeb, though this title could also refer to a Mughal Commander, appointed for that particular campaign, or even the Emperor's son, Prince Akbar (not to be confused with the famous Emperor Akbar in the times of Pratap). In the letter, the Marahana requests to be informed of the movements of the Mughal army in their march towards Gogunda which was headed by Aurangzeb's son, Prince Akbar. Prince Ram Singh was given charge of the safety of Udaipur Ghata (hilly range) which included the Arravalli Hills in Gogunda.

Ram Singh of Gogunda wanted to conclude the matter amicably and sought to meet the Nawab in charge of Prince Akbar's army to negotiate. Again the Khyat does not mention the Nawab by name but in this case it has to refer to a Mughal Commander and not to Prince Akbar, the Emperor's son who was leading the expedition. The Nawab agreed and a meeting was arranged. Ram Singh was accompanied by nine valiant Elders. The Nawab came with fifteen men on horseback. The two parties greeted each other and appeared to speak amicably beneath a tree for a while. At one point, to speed things along, as a pretext, Ram Singh expressed the desire to see the Nawab's sword. He then took the Nawab's sword and attempted to strike the Nawab. The Nawab defended himself and there was a great assault. Ram Singh was wounded as well as were the others in his party whilst three of the Elders were killed. But just as many were wounded and killed on the Mughal side too. The brave hand of Ram Singh killed the Nawab. The remaining soldiers of the Nawab scattered and fled in terror towards Godwar (the border of Marwar).

Jai Singh of Mewar was happy to hear about the splendid victory and gave Prince Ram Singh of Gogunda the Turban with the proper honour due. However, Jai of Mewar had not been a powerful ruler and preferred to be occupied with domestic affairs instead. Were it not for the fact that he ordered the construction of the now world famous Jaisamand Lake, named after him, he would not otherwise have been remembered.

The dates of the reign of the rulers of Mewar and the rulers of Gogunda from the late 1690s to 1751 coincide too much to make it plausible that the rulers of both of these kingdoms could have reigned and died, all three in succession at exactly the same parallel time. It is more likely that the people who set down the history in the Khyat, written a century later, took the more renown dates from the Mewar dynasty and applied them to the obscure ones of Gogunda. Therefore it remains unknown when Ram, Ajai, and Kanah II of Gogunda reigned exactly. What is known is that Amar II, Sangram II and Pratrap II of Mewar reigned alongside the three above mentioned Rajas of Gogunda. One of these facts that makes this feasible is that Ram's daughter of Gogunda married Amar II of Mewar in 1683 when Amar II was not yet crowned.

Amar II of Mewar had been as an undisciplined son as Jai had been an ineffective father and spent most of his life in exile as a troublemaker. In 1700, Amar was crowned at Udaipur at a time when the Mewar's treasury was empty. Since the main aggressor, Aurangzeb, had retired because of old age, Amar made unsuccessful attempts, that he could not afford, to conquer Southern India.

In this period, however, the Mewari painters were able to develop and perfect their art. Although it is known that painting existed in Mewar since the 1250s, this particular Indian Miniature painting, the characteristic of Mewari painting, developed and continued to do so through the reigns of Pratap I which ended in 1597 and endured without interruption up to the present day.

The technique employed by the Mewar artists was by the use of a single hair taken from the throat or tail of a squirrel in executing the detailed work of these extraordinary paintings. The Mewar paintings can be distinguished from the rest of Rajasthani art because they usually depict emotional situations through the use of simple bright colours, and like most of Indian history, all totally anonymous. It was Jagat II of Mewar 1734-1751 who encouraged painters to initial their work so that individual painters could be recognised.

In his reign, Amar II of Mewar added the Shiv Prasana to the City Palace (the Garden Palace known as Amar Mahal), verandas on both sides of the first entrance gateway with cupolas of Ghariyal a ceremonial bell which is rung, and where the drums are sounded. He died at the age of thirty-eight in 1710.

Ram too of Gogunda, is said to have died in 1710 but had reigned ten more years than his counterpart in Mewar, therefore placing Ram's coronation at Gogunda in 1689 giving him a reign of twenty-one years. Both rulers were also beset with family struggles. But while his counterpart Amar in Mewar had been a rebellious soul in his youth giving his father more than a few problems, Ram of Gogunda, was having problems with being a father.

Raja Ram of Gogunda had two sons; Vagat, who although was younger than Ajay, nevertheless got preferential treatment. Ram even tried to injure his oldest son and prevent him from coming to the throne since he had lost an eye, which reminds us of another Mewar predecessor, the Great Sanga, having a similar dilemma. With the death of Maharana Amar II in Mewar and the not too judicial in fatherly matters, Raja Ram of Gogunda, it was up to Amar's successor, Maharana Sangram II to settle the dispute between the quarrelling brothers at Gogunda.

Perhaps it was because the new Maharana bore the same name as that other Mewar Ruler for whom the law, that a mutilated Ruler could not take the throne had been waived- the Great Sangram at the time had in effect lost an eye, a hand and leg- not all in battle but in squabbling with his siblings- that the present Sangram ruled in favour of the elder, one-eye-less, Ajay, who thus became the 5th Raja of Gogunda Palace. However the Maharana did not leave the younger brother, destitute, but endowed Vagat with several villages, for what they were worth after such warring times. Perhaps Sangram II ruled so wisely not only from his sense of fairness but because in effect a deep bond of friendship had spontaneously developed between the Maharana and the Raja, as Ajai of Gogunda proved himself a great warrior and was faithful to the Maharana of Mewar Sangram II who rewarded him for his bravery. The dates of the reign of Mewar and Goguda are the same. It is possible that the these two Rulers were inseparable friends and the people who noted the history had placed them both reigning along side each other and thought best to let it remain so even in the time that was to come.

In 1734 Sangram II's son Jagat II inherits the Maharana's throne in Mewar and Ajai's son Kanah II inherits the Raja's throne in Gogunda. A similar relationship that had bound their fathers seemed to have been imparted to the sons too and Kanah proved as obedient to the Marahana as his father had been.

He is also shown to have been a great mediator, even though he may not have taken the right decisions all of the time. Kanah once punished the mountain people in Gogunda known as the Bhils as being responsible for a rebellion but it was more likely that all these aggressions were caused by the Marathas which had plagued the throne of Mewar during Jagat's II reign.

After centuries of fighting against Mewar, the Mughals, never could claim this kingdom as their own and the Rajput race of Rajasthan were never conquered by them. However, as Mughal power fizzled out throughout India which in 1806 with the death of Shah Alam brought a definite end to the Mughal dynasty, it opened the doors for aggression by an even more sinister power, that of the Marathas, Hindus like the Rajputs but unlike the Rajputs, ruthless, unscrupulous, wild and vicious ransacking every inch of Mewar soil. In 1736, during Maharana Jagat II's reign Maharatha Baji Rao captures Udaipur.

CHAPTER TWENTY

Marathan plunder of Mewar; British establish first Governor General in India, Warren Hastings; 1774 1ˢᵗ Maratha war; Maratha leader replaces Maharana at Mewar in 1782; 2ⁿᵈ war1803 and 3ʳᵈ war 1817; conspiracies among heirs to the throne of Mewar; Ratan, Maharana Raj II alleged son, supported by Choondawats Rajputs claims throne of Mewar against his uncle Ari who probably poisoned Raj II, leading to civil war; Jaswant II is driven from Gogunda by Ari and constructs Jaswant Garh; clashes between Choondawats and Skatavats Rajputs; Mewar is reduced to poverty; Col James Tod takes up residence as British Agent at the Maharana's court 1796; Maharana Swarup (1842-1861) has conflicting views with British Agents; Gogunda is robbed by a Minister of Maharana Bhim

Mewar, was now faced coping with hordes of Marathan terrorists demanding exorbitant payments in order not to have their lands annexed. Fate had reserved an ironical destiny for Mewar since the enemy had now become of the same race and creed, Hindus, like the Mewari themselves. In the forty years that followed Jagat's reign the Marathas drained Mewar Rulers of all resources until the British Government took over the discredited East Indian Company establishing their first Governor General, Warren Hasting in Calcutta, thus the first of the Maratha Wars began in 1774 and ending in 1782 with nothing much concluded in favour of Mewar but with the establishment of the Maratha Peshwa (leader) in place of the Marahana.

In 1803 the second war began due to the defeat of the Maratha leader and only lasted two years. The outcome was that after the first British success, the Marathas were left free to plunder Rajasthan and central India again. The third war, 1817-1818 resulted in the Maratha leader and his confederacy driven out of Mewar and Rajputana and his lands confiscated giving supremacy to the British.

Jagat II of Mewar, in spite of the Marathas' attacks was able to achieve the construction of Jag Niwas, which has since become the splendid white marble Lake Palace Hotel in Udaipur. Also, before dying however Kanah II of Gogunda married his daughter Jyot to a certain Dewlya Kunwar Samant Singh who, in 1768, constructed a splendid, magnificent temple in Gogunda, placing the statue of Lord Vishnu inside it. A small temple of Hanuman Ji was built near by.

With the Marathas' invasion as the background scene, Jagat II of Mewar in 1751 and Kanah II of Gogunda in 1754 depart from this world and their successors Pratap II of Mewar and Jaswant II of Gogunda take their thrones in such troubled times. Whereas Jaswant reigns in Gogunda until possibly another twenty-four years, Pratap II of Mewar dies two years later and his son Raj II takes the throne of Mewar in 1754 at the same time as Jaswant of Gogunda. The early death of Pratap II, he was only twenty-nine, supposes that he died in not altogether natural circumstances. This is no surprise, considering that on orders of his father, Pratap II was cast into prison because he had gifted Lakhola without his father, the Marahana's, permission.

With a father dying so young it is not surprising that his son and heir, Raj II was only eleven years old when he came to the throne and died, most likely murdered, seven years later in 1761 at the age of eighteen, without an heir. However, he did marry, borrowing money for the wedding as the protection money paid to the Marathas had left the Mewar Treasury completely empty. There is a painting in the museum of Udaipur which shows the barat procession of the ten year old Maharana Raj Singh II at his marriage in Gogunda to the daughter of Jaswant Singh II (Gogunda) in 1754. The next in line to the Mewar throne was Raj's uncle, Ari whom it is suspected was responsible for poisoning his nephew. Thus Ari II became the Mewar ruler in 1761 and reigned for twelve years until 1773 while Jaswant II of Gogunda was still on the throne.

As the Kingdom of Mewar was being torn apart by the Marathas and the internal struggle for power raged, Jaswant II of Gogunda had his own personal problems to solve. He was ordered by the Mewar ruler, Jagat II who was reigning at the time, to kill a certain Deora who had killed a certain Gosai who had tried to steal Deora's wife. There is also an episode which describes, Jaswant's bravery in killing a lion- a Rajput tradition to test the courage of a prince. But that's just in passing. However, it seemed quite curious that the people setting down the history in the Khyat thought it important enough to note.

At this point, the events now describe the succession to the Mewar throne after the death of the eighteen years old Raj II. The nobles hoped that Raj's wife, the daughter of a Gogunda Chieftan whose painting of the wedding is in the museum of Udaipur as mentioned earlier, was pregnant because the nobles did not wish to see the despicable uncle Ari on the throne. Raj's mother, fearing Ari's retaliation, said the wife was not pregnant so the nobles had to declare Ari the next Mewar Ruler. However, it is possible that Raj's young wife had indeed been pregnant because some time later, Ratan presents himself as the posthumous son of Raj II and claims the throne of Mewar. This led to civil war.

Ratan, supported by the Choondawats, (Choonda was Lakha's Crown Prince who was deprived of his rights of first born), installed himself in Kumbhalgarh. He also made a lucrative pact with the Maratha's chief for their support. Ari did no less, therefore there were Marathas and Mewari on one side, fighting for five years, Marathas and Mewari on the other side. At the same time in 1764 there was another famine to exhaust completely all resources in the Kingdom. Ratan's mother, Raj's Queen, claimed the throne of Udaipur for her son. Jaswant of Gogunda favoured Ratan, since the Pretender was Jaswant's own grandson.

Meanwhile, Ari tortured many Sardars therefore the Sardars and the Rani left the palace to take Ratan to safety. However, Ratan enjoyed life only briefly, but the Sardars did not disclose the young prince's death and crowned a substitute as king of Kumbhalgarh in place of Ratan. Led by the impersonator of Ratan, the Sardars attacked Ari in Udaipur; Jaswant of Gogunda also took part in this battle. The revolt was not successful and Jaswant had to succumb and seek Ari's pardon. But Ari was relentless in his persecution and tried to kill Jaswant at least three times, therefore Jaswant left Gogunda and took shelter in the surrounding small villages. One of these villages was Chuli-Dhani and it is here that in 1770, Jaswant's heir, Kunwar Shatrusall II was born. In 1772 Jaswant constructed a fort in Tarawali, in the Aravalli hills, now known as Jaswant Garh.

In 1772 the British Government took control of The East Indian Company and there was a respite of the civil war. The following year Maharana Ari went to Bundi to celebrate the spring festival where he was conveniently killed in a hunting accident organized by the Prince of Bundi.

Maharana Ari left two young sons, the eldest of which Hamir took the throne at the age of nine. This is considered Mewar's darkest moment. There were rivalry between the Shaktavats, descendants of a son of Udai

II, a brother of Pratap named Skati and the Chondavats, descendents of Choonda, Maharana Laka's first born who gave up his right to succession in favour of Mokal.

The succession of Ratan who was supported by the Chondavats was still pending. Hamir's mother, who was Regent, favoured the Skatavats. The Marathas taking advantage of this crises gained more territory from Mewar. Harmir died five years later in 1778, poisoned. His brother Bhim takes the throne at the age of ten.

In 1778 there is also a change of succession in Gogunda when Shatrusal II at the age of only seven, takes the throne at the death of his father Jaswant. Although there is no evidence to support either discord or friendship between the two kings, there is documentation that Bhim had much more direct dealings with Kunwar Lal, Shatrusal's son and heir who apparently was, as tradition demanded, the person to fight in place of the ruler. Their relentless enemy, the Marathas, attacked continuously. The inhabitants left their villages and Shatrusal left Gogunda for Jashwant Garh which the Marathas attacked but retreated.

The ruler of Mewar, Bhim was reduced to poverty by the Marathas until the British drove them back to Southern India after a series of wars. Thus in 1818 Mewar and all the States of Rajputana signed treaties with the British. In order to restore these kingdoms from their poverty, the British set up Agents and Col James Tod was the first agent to take up residence at the Maharana's Court. Col Tod, however, had known Bhim since 1796 and was not altogether convinced that Bhim was an efficient ruler, and even less a judicial father as he allowed his daughter to swallow poison to solve a marriage problem Bhim himself had caused since he was not able to agree on whom she should marry as he had promised her hand both to Maharana Bheem of Jodhpur but who on his death promised her to Maharaja Jagat Singh of Jaipur. Bheem's successor claimed the hand of Bhim's daughter or war. In order to avoid a diplomatic crisis Bhim ordered his daughter to swallow poison.

Nevertheless, under Bhim's reign, Mewar painting flourished and Chokha, the court artist was its major representative. Furthermore, Bhim had the famous Sun Window erected at Udaipur, where the Maharanas would show themselves to the people in troubled times. Meanwhile Shatrushal II in Gogunda came to the throne at the same time as Bhim in 1778 and was to reign for an inordinately long time. It is to be remembered he came to the throne at the age of seven and lived to an old age. It is recorded that he reigned for seventy-five years in Gogunda, a record in itself. The custom of the Talwar Bandhai was not celebrated at the time of Shatrushal's crowning since he was too young but was performed at a later stage under the order of Bhim Singh of Mewar where he received about fifteen villages.

During Shatrushal's reign the whole of Mewar was involved in wars against the Marathas in which Shatrushal took part in facing the enemy. Some of the traders and farmers fled from their villages and took refuge in Jaswant Garh. The Marathas demanded the people to surrender and pay the taxes and when their people did not surrender, the Marathas' army attacked. Raj Saheb, (Shatrusal II) fired against them and seeing their horses killed, the Marathas retreated and the people returned in safety to their villages.

The queen of Shatrusal II, Sisodiani Ji was interested in worship and ordered to construct a temple, Har Mandir, south of Gogunda where the statues of the god Ram were placed. She also ordered to construct a temple, Chatra Nath Mahadev eastwards to Gogunda near the road to Udaipur.

Another Queen of Shatrushal II, Chundawat Begu Ji was very interested in having a temple inside her residence, so Chatra Badaneshwar Mahadev was constructed by her inside the palace of Gogunda. The Chatra was named after the Queen and the idol of Lord Shiva was kept in the temple. The temple was completed in 1840. All such minor details carefully noted in the Khyat.

Meanwhile, long before the death of Shatrusal; at the age of sixty, in 1828, Bhim dies and is succeeded by Jawan, who, for the following ten years was to turn out just an ineffective Ruler as his father. Due to his life of debauchery and his relationship with a Nautch girl, (an entertainer) Jawan squandered the money the British had been able to recuperate for Mewar and died without an heir. However, like in his father's reign, Mewar painting flourished substituting the traditional Rajput style of hunts and courtly events with the more Western style portraits of eminent figures. Jawan had to adopt a son, he choose his cousin Sardar of the Bagore branch to succeed him.

Sardar was forty years old when he came to the throne of Mewar in 1838 and only reigned for four years in a climate of quarrels at court and the debt to the English increasing. Some of these local quarrels involved not only Mewar but also the court of Gogunda and Jodhpur as related above regarding Jaswant Garh. Sardar too was without an heir and adopted his younger brother Swarup.

At the time of Swarup's ascent to the throne of Mewar in 1842, Shatrusal II was still on the throne of Gogunda. Swarup was a judicious ruler whose priority on coming to the throne at the age of twenty-seven was to decrease the debt to the British which he did so partly, by cutting out expenditure at court. Nevertheless, he had his problems with the British. The new Agent was not understanding like Col Tod and expected Swarup to abandon some of the Rajput traditions, in particular that of sati, (widows burning themselves on their husband's funeral pyre), saying suicide was sinful.

Swarup refused, even though the Agent legally banned Sati in Mewar. The imposition of the British made Swarup despondent. However during the Indian Mutiny Swarup gave refuge in Jag Mandir to British women and children for which he received a personal thanks and invitation from Queen Victoria, which, however, he declined to visit and continued to refuse to comply with British dictates. His reign was constellated by conflict with the British, even unto death. As it was forbidden for his widows to commit Sati, a favourite concubine of his was drugged and persuaded to burn herself holding the Maharana in his arms, much to the displeasure of the British, of course.

Swarup 's heir, Shambhu, was also adopted. When Shambhu inherited the throne in 1861, Shatrushal of Gogunda had died eight years previously (1853) and his son Lal had taken the throne. However, throughout his father's reign Lal had many disputes that he was called upon to settle. These disputes involved several rebellions by the Bhils, mountain people against the Sardars who were allegedly the ruling people. Indeed, the beginning of the 19th Century, when Lal was a young Prince, was the period where the Marathas had the upper hand in all things in and around Mewar.

CHAPTER TWENTY ONE

The extraordinary adventures of Lal Singh of Gogunda b. 1793 d. 1863

Lal Singh of Gogunda in 1853 was sixty years old when he inherited the Raja throne in Gogunda. However the rebellions of the Bhils against the ruling people were so severe that the Talwar Bandhai (sword ceremony) given to the new king could not be performed at Lal's coronation- not only because of the dangers involved but also because there was no money in Mewar to perform such celebrations which during more prosperous times, are described at great length. It is noted without revealing too much, how the British Agents were called upon to settle the disputes but for some reason or other, the Agents changed most frequently.

Lal Singh was born in Gogunda in1793 when Maharana Bhim Singh was ruling over Mewar in Udaipur. In 1811 there was an outbreak of disputes in Potala (a village) and Kunwar Lal was sent to control the situation. Then the following year in 1812 there was a famine and drought which reduced the income of Mewar even further to 660 Rupees to manage the region, (about $23.00). One of the Ministers, Jodha Ram, requested to increase the amount because it was not sufficient but the only answer he got from Bhim Singh was to rob Gogunda.

Thus Jodha Ram took an army and marched towards Gogunda. Lal Singh was not in Gogunda at the time but as soon as he was informed he returned immediately. The army in Gogunda resisted the "enemy" for three days and prevented Jodha Ram to climb the valley. On his arrival in Gogunda, Lal Singh took seven men on horse back which were, four of his uncles and three devotees. He then marched towards the field where a furious battle was fought. Kunwar Lal attacked fiercely until the "enemy" retreated. Jodha Ram was wounded near the pond called Thoor. Then Lal Singh went to Udaipur and faced the Darbar but it is not known what passed between them- certainly Bhim Singh would think twice before considering another attack on Gogunda. It is interesting to note that at this time, Lal was only nineteen years old. It is even more interesting to note that even through famine and need, the Maharana of Mewar was able to set up an army to fight against his own right hand charge, Gogunda- hence cancelling themselves out and depleting even further any resources that were available, but such are the consequences of civil war and the futility of foolish men.

Three years later in 1815, another attempt to ransack Gogunda was made. Some Bhomyas, probably aided by Marathas, drove away a number of animals from Gogunda, but Lal burnt their villages and recovered the animals.

Meanwhile in Udaipur the Marathas robbed some shops. After they took the goods, they ran away and were not caught. Lal Singh was informed of this and immediately he set out with a number of men and caught them near Sayra. The three leaders with him were given titles by the king of Udaipur whilst Lal was awarded the honour of "Dari Khan-ka-Bida" which is the honour of being presented a betel leaf and the hilt of a sword officially at court. Therefore Lal Sigh was rewarded for his bravery. One wonders at this point who was keeping Mewar from falling to pieces, Maharana Bhim, or Crown Prince of Gogunda, Lal. It seems Col. Tod's character study on this Maharana is to be taken as being quite accurate.

When the Bhomyas of Bhomat refused to deposit the Khiraj which is a tax duty, Lal Singh was ordered to go and settle the dispute which he did so. He also went to settle disputes in Juda, Jawas, and Panarva which he did through negotiation or force and burning the villages when the Bhomyas refused to return the animals they stole from Gogunda. However, whichever means he used, Lal was able to establish peace in the area.

Previously to the above, the events around 1835 when Jawan I of Udaipur came to visit Gogunda, are well noted. It is quoted that on the first occasion he stayed for eight days and on the next, he stayed three days. Jawan was given a warm welcome and the Maharana, pleased to see such welcome and respect gifted Chippa villa as the seal made on this occasion verifies. The second time Jawan came to Gogunda it was on the event of attending the marriage of a chieftan and on that occasion the Maharana announced a reduction in taxes which for Gogunda was a great relief in those troubled times.

Three years later, in 1838, Jawan died and as stated above, Sardar from Bagore, was crowned sixty-ninth ruler of Mewar at the age of forty.

During his four year rein the debt to the British increased voraciously and quarrels abounded profusely. One of these quarrels involved Lal Singh. At court there was a certain Rao Dulha Singh who was envious of Kunwal Lal. The antagonism was so strong that Dulha schemed up a plan to trap Lal and make his father, Shatrusal I ban Lal from court. He persuaded a Brahmin, which is a member of the priestly class, to shape the plan. Dulha asked the Brahmin to go and request Lal Singh to perform some mantras, which is a form of enchantment because a royal son, Kunwar Khuman Ji who had been suffering from some illness was not well. It was a conspiracy and much to the shame of the Brahmin, he agreed to put the plot into action. When the Brahmin went to Lal Singh with his request, the Prince was not aware of the conspiracy and agreed to perform some mantras for the sick child.

The Brahmin took another person with him, Manik Chand and brought the materials, essences and drugs which are essential in the performance of the art of black magic. They went to Pichhola Lake in Udaipur and started some enchantment. They were chanting mantras according to the plan when some soldiers of Dulha Singh appeared and caught the Brahmin and Manik chanting. The Brahamin said that he was sent by Kunwar Lal to use mantras against the Darbar, Lal's father, Shatrusal. The trick worked because Shatrusal got angry and ordered to remove Kunwar Lal from court.

At this point, Shatrusal asked Lal's son, Man Singh to be ruler of Gogunda. But Man Singh refused to overtake his father which angered the Darbar who decided to punish Lal further. He ordered his nobles to attack Kunwar Lal, but his nobles all got together and requested the Darbar to make sure that Lal was truly guilty of the crime the Darbar accussed him of. The attack was postponed but Lal was removed from succeeding to the throne.

A thorough investigation took place and it was discovered that the Kunwar had not requested to have the mantras chanted nor for himself, nor against the Darbar and that he had no knowledge of the conspiracy put into action by the envious Duhla. Duhla, in due course, was found to have been the artifice of the whole episode and guilty of a serious crime. The persons responsible for the investigation requested the Darbar to call Lal back to court and reinstate him with all the honour due to a Crown Prince.

Kunwar Lal was at Ganerav at that time. Some nobles were chosen to go and get him, but Kunwar Lal refused to go back with them or be present at the Darbar's court. Instead, he decided to go to Halvad in Gujarat. Meanwhile, the Darbar (title referred to Lal's father) visited Chatra Bhuj Ji, a temple of Lord Vishnu, to pay his homage. He then sent for Kunwar Lal again. The Darbar sent a letter written by Mehta Ram Singh which expressed sorrow by the Darbar for the misunderstanding which took place in 1839. In the second part of the letter, the place of meeting was mentioned. The Darbar would meet him at Gadbor village. Lal Singh was advised to forget the misunderstanding and meet his father with open mind. He was further advised to serve the state, Gogunda, as he had been serving for several years. The letter tried to remove all suspicion or mistrust created by the incident. This time, the Kunwar presented himself before the Darbar. The Darbar, realizing his mistake returned all the honours due to his son and gave Lal the sword again. Thus, Lal was made head of Gogunda.

At the time of these events, Sardar (1838-1842) was on the throne of Mewar and praised Kunwar Man Singh (Lal's son), because he refused the throne in place of his father which was a great sacrifice and showed he had true affection for his father. Sardar was very pleased with the events in Gogunda and asked Kunwar Lal to accompany him on a pilgrimage to Haridwar in Uttar Pradesh.

Lal said that his family was at Ganerav and he himself had no means to travel, so the Darbar (Sardar) gifted him 1,000 Rupees and some camels. This is not an indifferent sum when we consider that one of Bhim's ministers was ordered to rob Gogunda because just over half that sum (600 Rupees) was all that was available to administer the whole of the kingdom. It is to be remembered that one of the major criticisms made against Sardar was that the debt with the British increased beyond measure during his reign- however, sometimes it is hard to condemn Sardar's lavish spending. They both stayed at Chouki of Pushkar and Lal enjoyed the Darbar's company for some time and then the Darbar set out for Ganga and Lal came home.

Another episode worthy of note occurred in 1845 when Sardar's adopted heir, his younger brother Swarup who came to the throne in 1842, was ruling over Mewar and, as stated above, was much more judicial in his spending than his brother had been. Whether or not, Swarup 's parsimonious attitude towards expenditure had any bearing or not on this matter, it is not known; nevertheless, the fact remains that the Oswal Mahajans, which are a business community left Gogunda to inhabit a city nearby, thus making the already precarious economical condition of

Gogunda even worse. However, it seems that Lal comes to the rescue again and was able to influence them and persuade them to return to live in Gogunda, which they began to do so, in spite of the deplorable economic conditions.

The following year 1846, Sardargarh, a thikana of the Dodia Rajputs from Kathiawar, was captured by the Shaktawats. The Shaktawats were the descendants of Udai II rebellious second son, Sakta, who defected to the Mughals and the clan are the continuous rivals of the Chondawats, descendants of Lakha's Crown Prince Choonda who was deprived of his right to rule in favour of his younger step-brother Mokal. With the help of Lal Singh Sardargarh was regained and Dodias, the original rulers came back into power having removed the Shaktawat Chatar Singh, thus confirming Jorawar Singh Dodiya the right to rule over Sardargarh. At the same time the community of the Bhomiyas tried to rebel against the state. An army led by Lal Singh crushed the rebellion and as punishment their village was destroyed. The Bhils, who were a wild mountain people but who had accepted the Mewar chiefs as their lords and under normal conditions gave valuable service in defence and hunting, attempted to rebel against the Rajput Authority. This rebellion, with the leadership of Lal Singh was suppressed in 1848.

Curiously enough, it is noted that in 1851 Lal himself took part in a rebellion. With the Sardars, he took part in a revolt against the Mewar Ruler Swarup; probably because Swarup's demands for defence were many and financial rewards meagre.

Two years later, in 1853, Shatrusall II finally dies and Lal, the legitimate heir, takes the throne of Gogunda; however, without the ceremony of the Talwar Bandahai. It was said this was due to his participation in the rebellion of the Sardars against the ruler of Mewar, which by 1854 is almost resolved thanks to the aid of the British agent in the area, but most likely it was because, as mentioned above, there were no funds to be found anywhere in Mewar for celebrations. Ironically, Maharana Swarup does send a letter apologising that the Ceremony of the Sword cannot be organized at that moment and regrets for the delay in the custom of Talwar Bandhai. The Maharana writes two lines in praise of the Kunwar, (Man Singh). A certain Mokham Khamesra was the bearer of the parwana (document).

So important were traditions held that the Khyat goes to great length in accentuating such events. The Khyat sates that the ceremony of Talwar Bandhai was organized in 1861 when Shambhu Singh came to the throne of Mewar. Various jewels, pearls, ornaments, spices and animals were given in gift- quite an achievement at a time when Mewar had been drained by the Marathas of all valuables, however these being only the left overs after the wars with the Mughals- even if some of the more important gifts were presented in the written form of a "rukka" i.e. a note of promise. The rukka listed; an elephant, a string of pearl beads, a sword with a golden hilt. It is not known if this promise was fulfilled or not.

Thus, Lal received the ceremony of Talwar Bandhai in 1863, as fate would have it, the same year of his death. During this year a strike was called by Champa Lal, leader of the business men in opposition against the new Rulers that the English Agent had imposed on the village people. Everyone in the village became involved in the strike, even the more manual workers such as sweepers, washer-men joined the strike. Man Singh, the then Crown Prince of Gogunda; promised them that the British Ruler would not be imposed upon them. But the people were determined and under the leadership of Man Singh they went to Udaipur and protested with the Darbar who at that time was Shambhu Singh who had come to the throne at the death of Swarup in 1861. An agreement was reached with the Darbar and the strike was called off.

Shambhu was also from Bagore like his two predecessors. Shambhu's father was imprisoned because he had attempted to kill his uncle, Swarup; consequently Shambu became the Raja of Bagore at an early age. Then, just a month before dying, Swarup adopted him as his heir; Shambhu was not yet fourteen years of age at the time when he also became the Ruler of Mewar, therefore a council was set up to handle his affairs with the British on hand to keep the administration on a solid level. The British Agent at the time in Udaipur was Lieutenant Colonel Eden who promoted the reorganisation of the police force, the civil and criminal courts; furthermore, Eden constructed main roads. Even though the involvement of the British was regarded as interference, Mewar benefited from the improvements made by Eden and when Shambu came of age to rule, Mewar's finances were much more solid than they had been in the past.

Up until taking possession of the throne, Shambhu had led a life of debauchery, instigated by those courtiers who wanted to take advantage of his vulnerability of youth. Yet, as soon as he became the legal ruler, Shambhu began to take his role of Maharana seriously. Although he could neither read or write, Shambhu appreciated the need for education. He was the first of his family to learn English and built schools for Mewar's youth; including, in 1866, the first school for girls. For the care he showed for his subjects, Queen Victoria decorated him in 1871. His memorable achievement however, was the construction of Shambhu Niwas Palace, adjacent to the Southern part of the City Palace in Udaipur which became the private residence of Arvind Singh, the present occupant on the throne of Mewar.

CHAPTER TWENTY TWO

The Khyat ends with mainly domestic events regarding Gogunda and the Kingdom of Mewar; British influence and the final decline of the Princely States after the Union of India: the present endeavours to make known what had been for centuries left unknown.

In 1863, two years after Shambhu was adopted heir to the throne of Mewar, Man Singh became ruler of Gogunda after the death of his father Lal Singh. After Man Singh went to offer his condolences on a death at court in Udaipur the ceremony of Man Singh's Talwar Bandhai took place in 1864. Maharana Shambhu attended the ceremony and so did various nobles. Kunwar Ajay Singh, Gogunda's Crown Prince, Man Singh's heir, was also present.

The Khyat which is fitting to recall is 'the book of Gogunda', states of a furious robbery of land that took place in Gogunda by the Bhomiyas, at this stage. A certain Rao Ji Jora Singh was held responsible for that robbery and an attempt to settle the matter with the aid of the English Officer, Captain Mukin, was made.

The boundaries of the disputed land were marked from the north Vaguni Pond to Vaguni Gogunda. The boundary was marked from the wall of the pond southwards. But agreement could not have been reached because the English Agent was shortly replaced by another, a certain Habad who took up the duties of the previous officer and tried to settle the dispute, but obviously, unsuccessfully because he too was transferred and Charles Oheg, a new officer was sent there. The dispute became even greater. The Bhomiyas were not satisfied with the area of the land given to them. Many other Officers came and tried to settle the matter.

Finally, a solution was found and it was decided to construct minarets to mark the boundary. Memad Khan and Lala Ganga Prasad were sent to decide the place where to position the minarets- the village of Juda was charged the expense of the minarets.

There was also a dispute of the Brahmins of Semtal. The Darbar gifted the village of Semtal to this Religious community, but they, the Brahmins were not prepared to give any kind of money for this- the outcome of which, remains unknown.

Added to these problems, there was a drought in 1868 in Gogunda and consequently a famine. Not a drop of rain fell during the otherwise rainy months of the season. The crop fields dried up and more disease struck the area; there was not a single home where smallpox did not claim some victim. It was due to famine that many left their homes. Bread and wheat were being sold at very high prices, even sugar was very costly. In misery, Mewar shed bitter tears, states the Khyat. Disease began to spread even further, due to starvation many left their homes. Those who did not leave died of fever. Cholera, tuberculosis and small pox spread relentlessly. Somehow, Maharana Shambhu Singh managed to provide food and ordered to prepare boiled wheat for the villagers.

Three years later, in 1871 a meeting of the Jagirdars who were the local landlords was organized. The Maharaj of Bhinder, Hamer Singh called the meeting. The meeting was probably called in order to establish the importance or precedence given to a Jagir since the dispute which followed was due to the fact that the precedence of Ganerav which was at number five was not respected. Bhinder, which was the capital of the Saktawt clan, was placed at thirteen but claimed to have priority over Ganerav. And because this order was not respected, a great dispute erupted in which many Sardars took part. The outcome, as is quite normal in such circumstances, is left suspended and it was not known what came of this event.

What is noted, however is that there was a welcome given to the Raj Rana of Patan in Gujarat when he visited Udaipur. With the Darbar Shambhu, Man Sing of Gogunda were present. The place of meeting was at the Inn of Teli which is now the B.N. College. The Nazrana (presentation of gifts) celebration took place and the Rulers of the following Thikanas (Capital of the kingdom) were present: the Rulers of Salumber, Delwara, Gogunda and Kanod. The Raj Rana was accompanied by sixteen of his Sardars, thirteen elephants, four hundred men mounted on horses, and two thousand cannons. There were cannon firings in honour of the Raj Rana (of Patan).

On the second day Raj Rana visited Shambhu Niwas with an elephant, two horses and one string of pearls- so the Khyat informs. He enjoyed some performances given by trained horses and elephants. The Maharana of Udaipur gave him suitable respect and the Khyat describes the Raj Rana's affectionate greetings he had received in Udaipur. With the Darbar, he visited Jagmandir, Shambhu Prakash and many other popular, royal palaces.

There is a note that in 1873 the Maharana, along with his queen, visited Chatra Bhoj- the tomb of the second ruler of the Guhilot Dynasty about 603-618 who was the son of Guhil, forerunner of the Mewar Dynasty.

Shambhu died in 1874 at the early age of twenty-seven. In his thirteen year rule he had become extremely popular and there were immense numbers of mourners which even caused riots in the streets. The British had to use all the powers they possessed to stop the distress afflicted ladies of the court from committing mass sati. Dying so young it was natural to suspect he had been poisoned, but an autopsy made by the British showed no sign of poison and it was likely that his earlier dissipated way of life had produced its adverse effects. Quite early in his reign, as Shambhu had no son, and was not likely to have one, the British assured a succession by exhorting Shambhu to elect an heir. This adopted son was his cousin, Sajjan Singh.

Sajjan Singh was only fifteen when he inherited the throne but his coronation was delayed for two years due to his uncle's, Sohan Singh of Bagor, opposition. Samarth Singh who was the father of Sajjan, had two brothers, Sohan and Sagat. Sagat was the older brother and was ruling over Bagor but for some reason that has not been recorded, during Shambhu's reign Sagat was removed and the throne and rights were given to Sohan. Sohan claimed that the holy men had predicted the date for the coronation was not favourable.

The British Agent at the time, Lieutenant-Colonel Wright asked the Brahaman astrologers to re-read the horoscope and this time they concluded that the date for the coronation was perfect. However, Sohan refused to give his alligence. This required the army of Mewar to march towards Bagor. A Note of Promise was sent to Man Singh in Gogunda ordering him to take part with his soldiers in the army of Mewar. The note mentioned that Bagor was sending troops to attack Mewar. The Darbar, Maharana of Udaipur, demanded some horses and Rajputs from Man Singh, artillery was also demanded.

The army of Mewar was sent to attack Bagor. At the time there was a heavy rainfall therefore the army could not go forward, thus it stopped for some time until the rain appeased and then went forward. Sohan Singh surrendered and he was taken to Udaipur where he was imprisoned and then banished. Man Singh, the Ruler of Gogunda, fought bravely and Bagor was restored to Maharaj Sagat Singh, the elder brother.

The rainfall that occurred is described in some detail. It had rained heavily for eight days and there were floods everywhere. Many animals and villages were destroyed and many people became homeless. All things in the houses were floating, there was a great loss of property and many people drowned. The Pond of Ranelav in Gogunda was flooded and there were eruptions in the walls of the pond. Two Rupees were collected from each household to repair the pond and even the Government made a contribution. By 1879 everything subsided.

Sajjan Singh was a handsome and proud Rajput who during his brief ten years reign had achieved many improvements in road and other public works constructions. He was concerned about judicial and education reforms. He built Sjjan Niwas Garden and Victoria Hall- an oasis of shady trees and a zoo. He also built Shikarbadi Hunting Lodge Sanjjangarh, commonly known as the monsoon palace which is now, unfortunately, in disuse. He was a lover of history and philosophy and founded the Sajjan Vani Vilas Library and a History Department. He commissioned the author Shayamal Das to write a History of Mewar, known as the celebrated Vir Vinod. He also requested the people of this area to set down a History of Gogunda, known as the "Khyat". Therefore the details mentioned in the Khyat which is one of the sources of this history was compiled on request of Sajjan Singh. Unfortunately, Sajjan Singh also indulged in alcohol and opium and possible an exaggerated use of these elements was the cause of his early death at the age of twenty-five.

Fateh Singh who was in fact six years older than Sajjan was the biological son of Dal Singh of Shivrati and had already been adopted by his elder brother Gaj at the time Sajjan Singh adopted him as his successor. The choice of a successor involved the opinion of many ruling families, Sardars and it is not to be excluded that the British would have had a say in the matter. However, the choice finally fell on Fateh. He was thirty-two when he came to the throne of Mewar and reigned for a memorable forty-six years.

At the time of the coronation of Fateh Singh in 1884, Man Singh was on the throne in Gogunda and was one of the Umaros present at the ceremony. The Umaros were the heads or kings of states within the Kingdom of Mewar. At that time the number recorded in the Khyat was seventeen, at present there are twenty-two. Sajjan's wish, when he requested that a history of Gogunda be compiled, was that traditions and habits be noted. Therefore a list of gifts and the names of the Sardars and guests present at an important event are recorded; the ceremonial etiquette and behaviour of Ruler and subjects when the Darbar of Udaipur visited Gogunda on any special event, a death, a coronation, a marriage.

The marriage of the Crown Prince's daughter in 1885 is recorded at length. The Crown Prince of Gogunda was Ajay Singh II, his daughter, Zhala Gulab Kunwar was married to Thakur Kesar Singh who was the grandson of the Ruler of Badnor. The Sardars from different Thikanas came to attend the marriage. They were from Delwara, Thana, Sardar Garh and Bhinder. It shows that Gogunda maintained good relationships with the other rulers. The marriage took place in the Hindu month of Phagun which is February to March. Near three to four thousand people attended the marriage, the major Sardars were present. It was noted, the marriage party arrived on time.

Man Singh, the Raja of Gogunda, his Crown Prince Ajay and younger son Prithvi went forward to welcome the marriage party. Many horses and elephants and camels were there along with the major Sardars. Grass, wood and stakes were collected, the big store houses were busy, they were full of clothes. Different supplies were kept in different store-houses. There is a long list of the essential supplies which were accumulated for the wedding, among which, many spices. This long list and their quantity is given in full in the Khyat. The blessed ointments and other ceremonial effects used in the performance of the marriage; the sweet dishes and delicious items prepared for the meal were also mentioned. The marriage party stayed for five days. Dresses, turbans, and valuable gifts were given to the members of the marriage party who were made most welcome.

Another motive for celebration recorded in 1885 is the visit of Maharana Fateh Singh, the new Ruler of Mewar. He was a keen hunter and came for that purpose to Gogunda as it was his desire to hunt a lion. The Raja of Gogunda, Man Singh and the Crown Prince Ajay, went to the village Bandrawade to receive Fateh Singh who came from Udaipur. Man Singh and Ajay greeted the Darbar and presented him with a Najrana, which consisted of two rupees each. It was customary to offer a gift to the guest. The Darbar took his food there and the next day they set out for Gogunda. At the time of the Darbar stay in Gogunda, he was presented with some valuable items and a feast was also prepared. The Chhadir and Halkara (men in waiting to the Maharana) were also offered gifts by the Thikana of Gogunda which shows how eager the people were to please the Maharana whom they considered with high esteem. Then the ceremonial party moved to the roof top of the palace where the feast was arranged.

As Fateh Singh had expressed, his first desire was to hunt a lion or any wild beast in a royal hunting game. He tried hunting in the forest of Jaswant Garh, but as he could not find a lion, he came across a boar and killed it. Then the Maharana left the Rawala (palace) and started out on his journey with a thousand men, four hundred horses, some elephants and camels. There were also some Sardars who accompanied the Maharana, poets and men in waiting.

In 1886, a pilgrimage made by the Ruler of Gogunda, Man Singh, is noted. Man Singh decided to set out for a short pilgrimage with his younger son, Kunwar Prithvi and Ajay's adopted son, Kunwar Zuzar. Some major personalities of Gogunda went along with Man Singh, his wife, Vagheli Ji also accompanied her husband. He took one hundred and fifty men and fifty horses with him- it was quite a procession. They made their first halt at Malwa, then they moved to Posina. Jhala Man Singh was warmly welcomed in Posina. He stayed at Posina for five days.

A Feast was arranged in their welcome, people in the village were invited to enjoy the special dishes. One thousand one hundred and forty five rupees was spent on it. (It is worth remembering that during the famine of 1812, six hundred and sixty rupees was set to manage the whole region.) Then he left the place with his procession including his wives and servants. He got into the train from "Bhomari", a railway station.

Man Singh enjoyed his journey with persons who had been the dominant figures of Thikanas. They made their stay at Sidhpur (a famous place for pilgrimage). Some preceptors were waiting at the station, the Lord and their companions paid their homage. Puna Ji and Gaya Ji (places of pilgrimage) were the holy places where Man Singh made his visit to offer the holy worship, of his ancestors and forefathers called Pinddan, a Hindu ritual, the holy worshipping of ancestors, at the bank of a holy river.

Man Singh was desirous to visit Ajmer and Pushkar, (Pushkar is a popular place for pilgrimages near Ajmer). He visited Pushkar and enjoyed the holy bath. It was the holy festival of Shivratri (festival of Lord Shiva), so Man Singh enjoyed it and gifted a piece of land to the priests. He returned to Ajmer, his son–in–law Badur Singh came to receive him, and a feast was arranged.

The singers received five rupees and the priests were gifted thirty rupees. He stayed in a famous inn, and then he moved to Jaipur. Next day he went sight-seeing. The procession of Man Singh stayed there for three days. Then they began their journey again. Bharatpur was their next stop.

Man Singh (Gogunda), enjoyed the beauty of the fort of Bharatpur, then he went to Mathura, the place where Lord Krishna was born. He made a holy-dip in the sacred river Yamuna, again he set out for Prayag Raj (a place for pilgrimage), Man Singh performed all the rituals there. He offered his worship there, and gave Dakshina (money offered to the preceptors and mentors).

Then he moved to Banaras, it is a place from where the sacred river Ganga flows. He offered his worship to Kashi Viswanath (temple of Lord Shiva) and Bheiravnath. The preceptors and mentors were presented money.

The Lord of Gogunda moved to Ayodhya, the place where Lord Ram, a Hindu god, was born. Then Man Singh went to the river Sarju for a holy dip. The visiting places of Raja Jhala Man Singh were Ram Mandir, Hanuman Mandir and Ghau–Ghat.

He left Ayodhya and set out for Lucknow and Haridwar, again he offered Pind-dan Puja. The Brahmins and priests, who helped worshipping, were gifted. They moved to Shahjahanabad, and Delhi.

Lal Kila, a Red-Fort, attracted him very much; again he went to the sacred river Yamuna for a holy-dip. He visited Baldan Gokul, Kshir-samundra, Mathura Girraj and Mansarovar. He halted at Bharatpur and Bandi-kui, and then he returned to Ajmer, again he took a holy bath in the Pushkar. There he got a message of sad demise of Badnor Bai,the death of Ajay's daughter. Shortly after Man Singh returned to Gogunda.

Man Singh was a generous and religious person. He got many temples repaired during his reign. In 1889 a temple of Lord Shiva Nilkanth at Kerva Devra, got a new shape. The Khyat states the name of the architect, who was appointed there, he came from Udaipur.

From this period onwards the following works of construction in Gogunda have been noted. The construction for a temple named Ummed Bihari Ji was started in 1887. Vagheli Ji Posina, Man Singh's wife took interest in the temple, due to her efforts it got its complete beauty in 1888 AD- in other words, that was when it was finished. Three thousand six hundred sixty six rupees were spent. Kothari Champalal, Daroga Bhai,

Gulab Singh and a builder named Ram Gopal were appointed to construct the temple.

The temple of Gulab shyam Ji was constructed in 1891. Raj Rana Ajay Singh was ruling that time. Five thousand rupees were spent on the construction.

The Kunwar Bagh-the garden of the son of a Rana at Gogunda which had already been deserted and left unattended, Raja Man Singh took interest in it and started looking after it. Later Kunwar Ajay Singh was gifted that garden. Man Singh ordered to enclose the garden with a wall, and then some plants were planted and a palace was built inside the garden.

This area of the palace, has been described as a labyrinth of steps, ramps and bent entries leads to the fourth innermost court, the Zenana Mahal (Women's Palace); which is the oldest part of the complex, originally erected by Man Singh (Shatrusal's father, who died at the battle of Haldighati in 1576), as a Mardana Palace (Men's Palace). The rectangular chowk (courtyard), was once occupied by a "formal" garden, and in the middle stands a small Mughal style Pavillian with cusped arcades. Separate apartments, now roofless are disposed on two levels all around, separated from one another by a high wall with concealed passage ways. Additional small dome Chhatries overlook the court from the higher levels. Some of these Chhatrias, (royal canopys over graves or Royal umbrellas), were built in the reign of Man Singh. Rana Man Singh was keen to have such monuments erected.

There are also several Chhatrias which have been built previously to commemorate an event in the past. Of these the Chhatri of Kheta Ji offers particular interest. This last Chhatri is not of the immediate Princely family of Gogunda but is a memorial of a medieval event. Maharana Kheta was the second ruler of Mewar to be given that title, his father Hamir, was the first. He was the father of Lakha and reigned from 1366 to 1382. His son Lakha was not the only one to have problems with his in-laws, because it seems that Kheta's father-in-law, Lal Singh murdered Kheta in battle and Lal's daughter, being the wife of Kheta committed Sati. This event must have had an effect on the people of Gogunda since the Chhatri was built in memory of the Queen who burnt herself on the funeral pyre of her husband. The temple site was the same place where she burnt herself. Holy worship of the Memorial is still being performed.

Raj Rana Man Singh died in 1891 as written on the Chhatri. He died of a minor ailment. He was a true worshipper of the Almighty God and till death, he had been chanting the name of God. Kunwar Ajay Singh, was present at the time of his death, he performed all solemnity. Tulsi leaves (a holy plant, basil) and Ganga Jal (Holy water of the sacred river Ganga) were put in his mouth.

The Khyat states that Raj Rana Man Singh had sharp memory and remained as he was till death. It also mentions the daily routine of Raj Rana Man Singh. It was his habit to spend over four hours in worshipping and praying Madbhagwat Gita and Bhagwat (religious scripture or books of Hindu). They were his favourite books and he read them daily. Many Sardars came to Gogunda at the time of the death of Man Singh to express their condolences. Following the Sardars were also major personalities from different Thikanas who came to Gogunda. The Khyat states the name of the Sardars and some dominant figures. The Khyat tries to show the relationship of the Thikana (Gogunda) with the other forty one Thikanas and to demonstrate how popular the Thikana was.

Kunwar Ajay Singh granted two thousand rupees, grains and twenty five cows for charity. His father, Man Singh, was cremated the same day and a hand of Ash was taken to Haridwar.

The Khyat states that Raj Rana Ajay Singh was also a religious and generous personality like his father. He inherited the throne in 1891.

The celebration of Chatra was performed near by the Kothar (storehouse) of the palace. Raj Rana's uncle Devi Singh, invited Ajay Singh to sit on the throne. Curd and green grass were presented him for good omen.

Bhawani Singh who was looking after the Fort of Jashwant Garh, Marked Tilak (holy symbol on the forehead). Raj Rana Devi Singh and all the servants of the Thikana presented many valuable gifts.

Having finished the coronation ceremony Ajay Singh went to the temple of Laxmi Narayan (Lord Vishnu) and Admata Ji for worshipping, and then he returned home and touched the feet of his mother Vagheli Ji.

Thakurani Bagadi Jetawat (his wife) was also a generous lady. The daughters born of this couple were Gulab Kunwar, who died soon in the early age. Bhag Kunwar Bai and Kishore Kunwar Bai, Kishore Kunwar Bai died in their childhood too.

In the same year 1891, Ajay's wife also left this world, when Ajay Singh was only 52 in age at that time. So, many Sardars insisted him to marry again, but he refused it. He was a very religious person and he had no charm in the worldly gains or lust. It was a matter of great sorrow that Kunwar Ajay Singh's only wife died. Kunwarani Jetawat belonged to

Bagadi, a Thikana in Marwar. The funeral and other rituals were performed according to the Rajput Hitkarini Sabha, which was established in 1887. A handful of Ash was taken to Haridwar, to flow in the holy river Ganga.

The coronation ceremony was performed according to the scriptures (sacred books). It was a happy occasion and everybody rejoiced to hear about it. A procession and gun firing were arranged to express joy, then Ajay Singh accompanied by fifty horses moved to Jaswant Garh. The new king went through some rituals. They were served opium at Jaswant Garh. After staying some time, they returned to Gogunda. Again he was warmly welcomed with Mashals (torches) in Gogunda.

Raj Rana Ajay Singh set out for Udaipur with his Lawajama (accessories, supplies and soldiers) for the Talwar Bandhai, sword ceremony in 1891. The Khyat listed the items which were taken with them and includes: a skilled horse, fifty other horses, 12 camels, four silver sticks, ornaments for the horses and was accompanied by two hundred and twenty five people.

The Talwar Bandhai was celebrated when Maharana Fateh Singh was ruling over Mewar. With the sound of trumpets and drums, Ajay Singh appeared in the Haveli at Udaipur. He was well dressed; a turban, royal belt and some ornaments enhanced his appearance.

Then a servant came to provide information that the Darbar was about to appear, Purohit Akhenath arrived; he was the personal priest to the Darbar. Maharana Fateh Singh came there a little later. Fateh Singh removed the cloth which was on the head of Ajay Singh, and took his place then the officials also took their places. The Darbar was presented with the camphor and betel and the ancient rituals were performed.

It is interesting to note that in the customary usage of offering gifts a cloth made of velvet to wrap around the body as a sign of good omen was given alongside sixty rupees of opium two rupees for the drum player and twenty five rupees was given to charity. The Khyat describes the dress, which was made for the new Lord at the time of Talwar Bandhai; a pag (turban), a white Dupatta (scarf like), a long white dress in the shape of a cloak.

Kunwar Bhopal Singh, Maharaja Gaj Singh, Zuzar Singh, and Prithvi Singh accompanied Ajay Singh. Prithvi was Ajay's brother, Zuzar his adopted son and the others were elderly relatives.

A list of some of the prominent figures present at the ceremony is made and indicates the places given to them according to rank. Pearls in the shape of rice were presented, curd green grass and many things, which are used for good wishes were offered him. A string of pearl beads was presented, then a sword made of gold, with a velvet Myan (a sheath). Nazrana (ritual of gift) was also made to Kunwar Zuzar. Many other Nazranas were performed. Several pages regarding the money spent on Nazranas were set down in the book.

Dhai Bhai Chatra Bhuj and Kothari Champa Lal stood with the Raj Rana till the ceremony was over. Again betel with camphor was served then Raj Rana Ajay Singh went to the palace of Gogunda. The Sardars who attended the ceremony also retired to their individual Hawelis. According to the custom, he gave his respects to the Rani (Queen) of Mewar, and then he went to the popular temple Jagdish Mandir.

Ajay Singh contributed to the beauty of the palace of Gogunda. During his reign which began in 1891, the palace got a new look, he made some changes in the palace. The palace required stairs. Ajay Singh was conscious about that and provided the facility. The stairs in the palace were ready, during the administration of Ajay Singh. When the Khyat states that the palace got a new shape, it is referring to the new complex built north-west of the palace and named after the Ruler, Ajay Niwas. The money spent was 4,096 Rupees.

In 1892 Kunwar Zuzar Singh (Ajay's adopted son) got a palace built. The name of the palace was Zuzar Niwas. Though the Khyat does not give actual location, but it can be estimated that it had been a part inside or around the original palace. Money spent on it was 4,000 Rupees.

Ajay Singh took interest in the Temple of Jyot Shyam Ji and he ordered to reconstruct it in 1894.

The Khyat mentions the earthwake which affected the Middle East and the north part of India. This earthquake started from Rajasthan then Mathura, Delhi, Ajamgarh, Gorakhpur, Chhapra, Darbanga, and Calcutta was affected by it. Many houses collapsed. It was a great loss to mankind and a great terror could be seen every where. The buildings of Trail Company, Por Company and the office of a newspaper collapsed. Churches, temples, and many huge buildings were destroyed. Another earthquake affected Assam.

Then there is a mention of the death of well known personalities such as the death of the Ruler of Jodhpur, of Swami Bhaskaranand, a popular saint who died in 1899 and of Raj Rana Jalam Singh, ruler of Delwara who died in 1900.

The Nineteenth Century closes in 1899 with a dreadful famine. Men, women, animals, and each and everything became its victims. The English government and many Sardars helped the public by giving clothes, money, grains, and many things whatever necessary to survive. Corpses could be seen here there and everywhere. The rate of gold and silver silver went down.

The Khyat gives a list of ponds and wells in Gogunda. The Pond of Rane Rav was situated in the south of Gogunda. A Maharana of Udaipur ordered to dig it up, and it was dug in the year of 1423, this was the reign of Mokal 1421-1433 son of Lakha and the Rathore's daughter, thus establishing that some kind of structure which later became the palace was in exsistance even then.

About two scores of wells, constructed during the various reigns are noted also a small stream is described as running through the Ghata (cliffs) of Bhaodi, as being very beautiful. The name of that stream was Ruparel, a name given by Ajay Singh

It is noted that a huge DariKhana was constructed where the king and the courtiers assembled and discussed important matters. The name of that Darikhana was Dam Dama. It mentions that the Fort of Jaswant Garh was situated near the village Tarawali and that Seth Jeting Ji received a Rahat in Jaswant Garh which is a piece of land with appliance for lifting water from a well. A Thana was constructed by Raj Rana Jashwant Singh which is a building similar to a house and was constructed in Mal-ka-Thana.

There is a mention of Dholengar Parbat and is described as a very splendid mountain, located near Gogunda. The Garda Magra Hills are mentioned for their fame and because the mountain of Gadra drew the Boundary of Gogunda. Other hills located north of Gogunda are the Khaman Hills and the Hills of Mazawad.

Since Gogunda abounds in temples, the Khyat ends its poem with a description of about twenty-six temples, the reason for their construction. It is noted for example that the Temples of Brahma Ji, Bheru Ji, and the temple of Shiva in Rawla, were very popular. The Temple of Shiva, known also as the blessed one is one of the triad of the Hindu gods namely Brahma, Vishnu and Shiva. Shiva represents the destructive and creative forces in the universe. He is shown entwined in snakes with a necklace of skulls when he represents the destructive forces; as the lord of creation he is shown as the phallic male symbol of fertility. In addition, Shiva is considered the god of asceticism and of art, in particular dance. He is depicted as dancing in a circle of fire which shook the cosmos and created the world. He holds a three-pronged spear, a third eye is placed in the middle of his forehead and his plaited hair has the goddess of the river Ganges in it. He is attributed to live in the Himalayas and rides on a bull called Nandi. The goddess Parvali is his beautiful consort. The god of Mewar, Lord EklingJi, is a manifestation of Shiva. This temple was inside the palace until the time of the last ruler Raja Rana, Jhala Himmat Singh whose consort bequeathed the temple to the people and thus, the Temple was left on the outside the newly constructed boundary wall.

Other famous temples in and around Gogunda were: in the Village of Vanoi the Temple of Bheru Ji, Village Samtal the Temple of Thakur Ji, Village Kachba the Temple of Charbuja and the Temple of Rameshwar Mahadev. Similarly the temple of Goddess Saraswati, the Temple of Ram Chandra Ji Goddess, the Temple of the Pipalaz Goddess, and the Temple of Gandaw were very popular temples. Some other temples were situated near Jaswant Garh and were very popular at that time.

Many temples of that time are still in their original form while some temples have been destroyed by the invaders or the elements of nature earthquake, wind, water and sun rays. But one can see their remnants.

This is as far as the Khyat takes the history of Gogunda, but a century later, there is nothing much vital to add; except, to write the word end to the oldest Monarchy in the world, that of Mewar; of its satellite, Gogunda and the Rajput race that were the protagonists. There remains the sense of achievement that the only history concerning Gogunda has been at last uncovered to reveal an unbroken Rajput blood line of succession from the Makwana people in Sindh, a thousand years ago to Sajja Singh who died in the 2nd sack of Chittor in 1534 and had fathered Gogunda's Royal lineage of the Jhala Rana Rajas drawing upon the Rajput race of the encompassing royal houses, rulers and warriors that interacted with one another.

After the death of Fateh of Mewar, a reign that lasted almost half a century, his crippled son Bhupal sits on the throne of Mewar from 1931 to 1955: crucial years; not only for Mewar, or for the whole of India, but for the entire world itself. Towards the end of World War II, the unrest in India was directed towards one aim, that India should be for the Indians. The British were in favour that this would be so and India became independent on 15th August 1947.

Bhupal agrees to become a part of the Indian Union, thus putting an end to the reign of the Indian Princely States. Nevertheless the neo-Indian Government promises to recognise the official titles of the Rulers and allocate an allowance from the Privy Purse for the maintenance of the Princely States. A promise which would be short lived and be dispensed with completely in 1969 when the Indian Government of the neo Indian

Republic abolishes the Privy Purse. Thus Bhupal's adopted son, Bhagwat Singh, a country boy whose natural father was Prince Pratap of Bhupalgarh, had more than one problem to solve as Ruler of Mewar.

He was the heir of palaces, forts, temples, and a host of servants; but no revenue for their maintenance. The buildings could not be left to deteriorate, the servants could not be thrown out- he found himself with three hundred dancing girls that his predecessor had kept- what could he do with them? Maharana Bhagwat decided to give them a reputable career and offered training as nurses, but they refused. Thus there was nothing else to do but keep them! Bhagwat sold some of his property to the government, some he turned to commercial use, and created the Maharana Mewar Foundation in order to preserve the history of the world's oldest ruling dynasty.

When the Indian government abolished all privileges in 1971 Bhagwat realized that the institution of Maharana would be lost for ever if he did nothing to safeguard it. Therefore, after much thought, in 1980, Bhagwat Singh bequeathed his whole estate to a trust which would become the Maharana Mewar Institution Trust, thus ensure the continuity of the State and the perpetuation of the institution of Maharana. However, his oldest son did not agree and demanded his share of the estate as heir. But Bhagwat was convinced that this was the only means to preserve what could be preserved of a glorious history and nominated his second son, Arvind, head of the Trust. Today, Arvind is the present Ruler of Mewar and due to this Trust he could very well claim to sign his name as Maharana, but prefers to be known as Arvind Singh Mewar.

The fate of the Palace of Gogunda was less fortunate. History records that after the death of Ajay Singh in 1901, his brother Prithvi is made Ruler of Gogunda as Ajay died without issue since it is probable all his children died in their youth. After Prithvi, Dalpat takes the throne and then Manohar. His son, Bhairo Singh, is known to have died on 27th July 1990 and was succeeded by his Crown Prince Himmat Singh who became the 16th and last Raja of Gogunda. His full title would have been Raja Rana Himmat Singh Jhala of Gogunda. But he and his heirs are simply granted the courteous title of Shri, which is a term used when addressing a honourable person, often used in appellation of a Deity.

Gogunda Palace and its dynasty endured the same plight of loss of title rank and revenue when the Indian Union was formed in 1947. Most of the family of the 15th Ruler of Gogunda, the late Raja Bhairo Singh, left the palace and sought a means of earning a living in the country shortly after the Independence of India. After the death of the Raja, his wife, Rani Budh Kanwar Sahiba, continued to live in the palace with only a few servants, as the queen, until the early 1990s.

During the British Rule, a part of Gogunda Palace, Anand Niwas, was restored in the British style.

But once the palace was no longer in use, it began to decline and deteriorated so fast that soon parts of the palace were reduced to ruins. Udai Niwas which was used as the Revenue Office was the first section to be completely destroyed and which the architect who restored the palace at the beginning of the 21st century had to design and construct a totally new building in the function of a hall.

The Dome Palace which was first, a Zenana- women's quarters, then a Mardana- men's quarters, later became the Residence of the Ruler. Opposite the Dome Palace the rectangular complex which is now the Zenana and stretches across the court yard next to the Ayurbedic Garden has loop holes for the use of guns, all along the exterior wall... a subtle reminder of the existence of Rajput warriors.

There is an indentation in the North corner of the boundary wall because the villagers had dismantled that part of the wall and taken the bricks to use elsewhere. The same fate occurred to the South part of the wall which was completely destroyed by the locals, using the bricks to build their own houses. Going around Gogunda, one can see the bricks of the boundary wall woven into the construction of the walls of some of the houses. The villagers occupied parts of the palace and removed anything which was not fixed such as doors and windows- they left, however, the two immense artillery cannons.

On the outside of the existing boundary wall, there are remnants that show there had been three boundary walls and confirms the records that Gogunda had once been an effective and strategic fortress, not only in the times of Pratap but previous Mewar rulers, even as far back as the reign of Kumbha, had utilized this Mewarian seat as a stronghold of defence. The destruction of these walls must have occurred during the vicious raids of the Marathas which took place after the end of the Mughal Empire.

The East Corner reveals a building that has no name but it was originally built with stones and mortar made of mud and cow dung. This part of the complex has been completely designed and constructed anew with the recent restoration made by the Italian architect Remo Serafin. This was undoubtedly the first part that had laid the foundation, so many hidden centuries away, of what was to become the Palace of Gogunda and the gateway that would unfold the concealed events of the encompassing Rajput Warriors.

APPENDIX

Summary of Simultaneous Rajput Rulers and their Contenders

A. MEWAR RAJPUT (Rajputana - Rajasthan)

B. MAKWANA RAJPUT KIRANTI (Sindh Pakistan) Ancestors of Jhala House Rajput: Raja Palace of Gogunda

C. SOLANKI RAJPUT (Gujarat)

D. PARAMARA RAJPUT MALWA (Pradesh)

E. SIMULTANEOUS FOREIGN RULE IN INDIA

A. MEWAR RAJPUT (Rajputana - Rajasthan)

Ruler	Dynasty	Capital
1st 569 GUHIL	**GUHILOT**	IDAR
2nd 603 BHOJ		Idar
3rd 615 MAHENDRA	Rebels take Idar-Gujarat	Idar
4th 626 NAGADITYA	Moves capital to	NAGDA
5th 646 SHILADITYA		Nagda
6th 661 APARAJIT		Nagda
7th 688-716 MAHENDRA		Nagda

Marries Maun Mori's sister (Ruler of Malwa). He was murdered by someone in the court leaving a three years old Crown Prince Kalbhoj in need of protection from both his uncle Maun Mori and the usurping assassin. He was taken to the hills and hidden by the Bhils where he lived as a cow herd and meets the sage Harit Rishi who prophesizes Kalbhoj would be the care taker for Lord Ekling (the real ruler) of a kingdom that would be named Mewar. He is also invested with a special sword which would lead him to the throne of Chittor. In fact when Kalbhoj arrived at Chittor The Ruler, Man Mori promised anyone who could sever the iron pillar situated there would be given half the kingdom of Mewar, which at the time was in the hands of Malwa.

There follows a lapse of 18 years.

8th 734-753 BAPPA RAWAL (KALBHOJ)	GUHILOT	CHITTOR

Founds the MEWAR Dynasty and takes CHITTOR from MALWA which he makes the capital

9th 753 KHUMAN I		CHITTOR
10th 773 MATTAT		Chittor
11th 793 BHERT PATT I		Chittor
12th 813 SINHA		Chittor

13th 828 KHUMAN II		Chittor
14th 853 MAHAYAK		Chittor
15th 878 KHUMAN III		Chittor
16th 942 BHERT PATT II		Chittor
17th 951-953 ALLAT		

Loses CHITTOR to SIYAKA II

Establishes new capital at   AHAR

961 Paramara Ruler, Raj of Malwa rules at Chittor

953-971 Possible INTERREGNUM

18th 971 NARWAHAN		AHAR
19th 973 SHALIWAHAN		Ahar
20th 977 SKAKTI KUMAR		Ahar
21st 993 AMBA PRASAD		Ahar

Fights with other Rajputs to overcome, unsuccessfully, Mahmud of Ghazni from Afghanistan who conquers Sind in 1005

22nd 1007 SHUCHI VERMA		Ahar
23rd 1021 NAR VERMA		Ahar
24th 1035 KEERTI VERMA		Ahar
25th 1051 YOGRAJ		Ahar
26th 1068 BAIRATH		Ahar
27th 1088 HANSPAL		Ahar
28th 1103 VAIRSINGH		Ahar
29th 1107 VIJAY		Ahar

CHITTOR taken from Malwa by Gujarat

30th 1127 ARI I		Ahar
31st 1138 CHAUD		Ahar
32nd 1148 VIKRAM I		Ahar
33rd 1158-1168 KARAN		Ahar

Family split, his son Mahap founds Dun kingdom, son RAHAP founds SISODIA Family

34th 1168 KSHEM	Ahar
35th 1172 SAMANT	DUNGARPUR (NAGDA)
36th 1179 KUMAR	Dungarpur (Nagda)
37th 1191 MATHAN – Rules from	Dungarpur (Nagda)
38th 1211 PADAM	Dungarpur (Nagda)
39th 1213-1253 JAITRA	CHITTOR

Nagda is destroyed by Iltutmish.
Jaitra defeats Malwa Rajput Ruler and makes CHITTOR the capital of Mewar again
1234 Defeats Sultan Iltutmish

1253-1261 Possible INTERREGNUM

40th 1261-1267 TEJ (Guhilot) rules from   Chittor

1267-1273 Possible INTERREGNUM

41st 1273-1302 SAMAR. Rules from   Chittor
His son Kumbh Karen migrates to Nepal.
1291 HAMIR Singh is born to Rana Laska's son, Ari, of Sisodia
(Successor of Rahap son of Karan I 1158-1168)

42nd 1302-1303 RATAN   Chittor
Allaudin fails to add Ratan's wife, Padmini to his harem.
January 1303- FIRST SIEGE OF CHITTOR
1303 ALA-UD-DIN CONQUERS RAJPUTANA
Rana Laska of Sisodia sends Ajay and two of his ten sons and grandson HAMIR (Crown Prince Ari's son) to Kelwara to safety. Ratan and all his family remaining are slaughtered.

1303-1326 HAMIR exile in Kelwara as Mewar is occupied by the Sultanate of Delhi.
Laska's son Ajay starts attacking Imperial strongholds
Ajay is killed in battle.
Nobles proclaim HAMIR Maharana

Ruler	Dynasty	Capital

43rd 1326-1364 MAHARANA HAMIR I SISODIAN   CHITTOR
The First **SISODIAN** Ruler and the first to use the title **MAHARANA**
Retakes Chittor

44th 1366-1382 KSHETRA   Chittor
2nd SISODIAN 1362 Takes Ajmer and Jaipur from Tughlugs. Defeated
Idar's Rao Ranmal (Rathore), regained Mandalgarh and the south east.
1382 Assinated by Hara chief of Banbaoda in a dispute of marriage.
Two of his sons from a concubine, Chacha and Mera, later assassinate
Kshetra's grandson.

46th Ruler MOKAL   Chittor

45th 1382-1421 LAKHA   Chittor
Retakes Mewar's provinces.
Marries Rao Ranmal's sister (Rathore) in place of his son Choonda who
loses his status of Primogenitor but nominated Regent.
Dies ousting Muslims from the holy city in the North East, Gaya.

46th 1421-1433 MOKAL aged 5   Chittor
Defeated Nagour's Firoz Khan, Gujarat's Ahmad Shah and the Delhi
Sultan at Raipur.
Constructed Rane Rav Pond, South of Gogunda.
His mother, Hansabai, deposes CHOONDA as Regent who retires to
Malwa.
Is murdered by Chacha and Mera, stepbrothers (Kshetra sons)

47th 1433-1468 KUMBHA aged 6   Chittor
Rao Ranmal Rathore (Hansabai's brother) kills Mokals murderers and
Choonda's brothers in an attempt to gain the throne of Mewar.
Hansabai asks Chunda to return as Regent, ousts invaders, and forms the
Chundawhat Clan.
Constructed Kumbhalgarh from an existing fortress (2nd Century AD)
and Reinforced Gogunda.
Defeated the combined forces of the Sultans of Gujarat and Malwa Builds
the Tower of Victory at Chittor to commemorate the battle.

He exiled his Crown Prince Raimal to Idar for supporting the fortune tellers who had predicted his death which was to be achieved by the hands of his younger son UDAI

48th 1468-1473 UDAI I   Chittor
Considered as illegitimate reign. Crown Prince Raimal comes back from exile with an army and claims the rightful throne.
Udai flees to Delhi to seek help from Buhlul but is fortuitously struck by lightning.

49th 1473-1509 RAIMAL   Chittor
Went into exile when his younger brother Udai murdered their father Kumbha and usurped the throne from Raimal. After Udai's mysterious death Raimal returned to take rightful possession of throne and gave refuge to **AJJA** and **SAJJA** whose throne in HALVAD had been usurped by their younger step-brother Rano Ji in 1499.
1475 Sultan GHIYAS-UD-DIN of Mandu (Malwa) attacks Chittor is defeated and retires to Mandu.
In later years the Sultan sends his general Jafar Khan but the Malwa forces are routed out of Mewar. During these raids, it is noted that **Ajja** and **Sajja** had a prime role in the defence of Mewar. Consequently Raimal gave Ajja the estate of Bari Sadri and DELWARA to SAJJA- Forerunner to the throne of Gogunda.

50th 1509-1527 SANGRAM (SANGA)   Chittor
A warrior, dismembered by wounds, was third in line to the throne which he took after his first two brothers Crown Prince Prithvi and Jaimal were killed.
Fights various wars against the Lodi SIKANDER and after 1517, the Mughal BABUR, of which he totals 18 victories. Under his reign, Mewar's power reached its peak, his greatest antagonist being Babur who had the upper hand at the battle of Khanwaha 15 March 1527 where Mewar's losses are immense.
1516 His crown Prince BHOJRAJ marries the poetess Princess of Merta, Mira Bai
1521 Bhojraj dies in battle Mira Bai is scandalized for not committing Sati
1522 UDAI, Sanga's youngest son is born and succeed the Maharana after the death of his two older brothers, Ratan and Vickram.

Sanga was probably poisoned so as to make an end to continuous taking up of arms.

51st 1527-1531 RATAN II   Chittor
Persecutes his widowed sister-in-law Mira Bai.
Kills and is killed by Surajmal Hada of bundi during a boar hunt.

52nd 1531- 1536 VIKRAMA SINGH II   Chittor
Ratan's younger brother was 14 when he came to the throne and was considered as insolent as his predecessor.
The Mughals took advantage of the weakness in the leadership of Mewar and attacked Chittor causing the 2rd Sack in 1534.
Vikram Fled to hillside after attack from Mughals but retained the throne even though Banbir was appointed Regent.
As Banbir was the son of Raimal's Crown Prince Prithvi, he resented the fact that his father's brother, Sanga got the throne and revenged himself by mudering Vickram while he was roistering with his concubines. Banbir then went in pursuit of Udai, who was next in line. But Udai escaped to Kumbhalgarh with his nurse Panna Dhai who sacrificed her own son in place of Udai.

53rd 1537-1572 UDAI SINGH II Capital: CHITTOR till 1568
                                             from 1570 - UDAIPUR
1537 Nobles discover the 15 years old Udai at Khumbhalgarh and proclaim him Ruler.
1540 Udai defeats Banbir at Malvi and returns to Chittor as new Maharana.
1562 Udai gives hospitality to Rulers who have rebelled against Akbar causing conflict.
1567 Udai builds Moti Mahal a temporary palace on the Pichola Lake which does not prevent Akbar from marching on Mewar and to save the royal family line Udai is urged to take refuge at GOGUNDA.
1567-8 AKBAR attacks and causes the 3RD SACK OF CHITTOR
Udai shifts his headquarters between KUMBHALGARH and GOGUNDA, finally chooses to found his new capital in Udaipur and begins construction of the City Palace in 1570.
Dies at Gogunda while visiting his son Pratap who had made his quarters there.

54th 1572-1597 PRATAP SINGH I   GOGUNDA

Born in Kumbhalgarh while his father Udai was in exile. Was raised in the rugged hills of the Aravalli in Gogunda and consequently won the trust of the Bhils (mountain people) who proved indispensable for his safety during the continuous attacks of Akbar especially at the battle of Haldighati.

At the age of 32 he is crowned at Gogunda, and makes it the capital of Mewar.

Reinforces forts including Gogunda.

BATTLE OF HALDI GHATI 18th June 1576

"No defeat more glorious.
No victory less noble."

Roll of honour:

In remembrance of the following who were killed:

Pratap's Chetak-mounted statue along with the statues of - Jhala Man, Bhilu Raja (the tribal chief), Bhama Shah, Hakim Khan Sur and an attendant-foot-soldier were placed in front of the Parliament House in New Delhi on August 21, 2007.

1578-9 The Mughals poison the waters in Kumbhalgarh forcing Pratap to remove his capital to Chavand. Mughals take possession of Kumbhalgarh and Gogunda continues to be under siege.

However, by 1582 Pratap regains his lost territories at the battle of Diwer (near Haldighati) under the command of his Crown Prince Amar.

55th 1597-1620 AMAR SINGH I   Udaipur

Negotiated Peace Treaty with Khurram (later Shah Jahan) at Gogunda 1615

Sends his son Karen to the Mughal court – Only compromise by the Mewar Rulers to the Mughal Oppression.

56th 1620-1628 KARAN SINGH II   Udaipur

Exchanged turbans with Salim's son Khurram (Shah Jahan) and signed a Peace Treaty with Prince Khurram at Gogunda in 1615.

Gifts many villages to Kanah of Gogunda in 1619 possibly for his investiture as Raja.

57th 1628-1653 JAGAT SINGH I   Udaipur
Encouraged the development of Rajput intricate miniature painting.
Begins the restoration of Chittorgarh.

58th 1653-1680 RAJ SINGH I   Udaipur
1658 Gives refuge at Kelwa (in Aravalli) to Rathores from Jodhpur who
wished to rebel from continuing to be under Aurangzeb's Mughal forces.
Breaks peace treaty of 1615 by reinforcing Chittor

59th 1680-1698 JAI SINGH   Udaipur
Orders Crown Prince Ram of Gogunda to fight against Aurangzeb's son,
Prince Akbar.
Was an ineffective father.

60th 1698-1710 AMAR SINGH II   Udaipur
Had spent most of his youth as a trouble maker in exile.
Failed in attempts to conquer southern India.
Mewar's Treasury empty.
Mewari painters develop their art.

61st 1710-1734 SANGRAM SINGH II   Udaipur
Settled the dispute of succession between the sons of Ram of Gogunda

62nd 1734-1751 JAGAT SINGH II   Udaipur
Marathas attack Mewar fiercely for the next 40 years draining Mewar's
resources completely.
Nevertheless he constructs Jag Niwas (now hotel).
Encourages painters to sign their works.

63rd 1751-1754 PRATAP SINGH II   Udaipur
Was imprisoned by his father.
Dies in mysterious circumstances at age of 29.

64th 1754-1761 RAJ SINGH II   Udaipur
Only 11 when he came to the throne.
Probably poisoned by his uncle and successor Ari, at the age of 18.
Borrowing money he married Jaswant II (Gogunda) daughter in 1754.
His probable son Ratan was born posthumously.

65th 1761-1773 ARI SINGH II   Udaipur

Probably poisoned his nephew Raj II and claimed the throne as no heir had yet been born to Raj.

Had extremely bad temper and was despised.

Ratan, the alleged posthumous son of Raj claimed the throne. This caused civil war.

Ari was killed in a hunting "accident" organized by the Prince of Bundi.

Was succeeded by his son.

66th 1773-1778 HAMIR SINGH II   Udaipur

Was only 9 when he came to the throne.

Died poisoned 5 years later in 1778.

His father Ari's widow, Sardar kanwa Jhali, a ruthless woman from Gogunda, was Regent.

The succession of Ratan still pending.

67th 1778-1828 BHIM SINGH   Udaipur

Hamir's brother and adopted heir.

Came to the throne at the age of ten.

Ari's widow still Regent.

1782 ends the first 8 years long war against the Marathas which established the Marathas' Peshwa in place of the Maharana.

Nevertheless Mewari painting flourished.

1818 **Col Tod** takes up residence at the Maharana's Palace as British Agent till 1822.

68th 1828-1838 JAWAN SINGH   Udaipur

Due to a life of debauchery, Bhim's son Jawan squandered what the British had been able to recuperate.

However Mewari Painting continued to develop substituting the traditional Rajput style of hunts and courtly events with the more western style portraits of eminent people.

69th 1838-1842 SARDAR SINGH   Udaipur

Sardar was Jawan's cousin and adopted heir.

He was 40 when he came to the throne.

He reigned only 4 years in a climate of quarrels not only in Mewar but with Jodhpur (Rathore) and Gogunda regarding the occupation of Jaswant Garh.

70th 1842-1861 SWARUP SINGH   Udaipur

Was Sardar's younger brother and adopted heir.

His policy was to cut costs to reduce debt to the British.

However he refused to implement British rules and maintained the custom of Sati.

Nevertheless, gave refuge to British women and children in Jag Mandir during the Indian Mutiny but refused to go to Queen Victoria's court for decoration.

1812 A great famine added to Mewar's problems.

71st 1861-1874 SHAMBHU SINGH   Udaipur

Was the son of Swarup's nephew (originally adopted heir) who was in prison for attempting to kill Swarup.

Shambhu was 14 when he came to the throne so his affairs was handled by the British Agent who at the time was Eden which made Mewar's finances more solid than they had been for a long time.

Until he became Maharana he lived a life of debauchery but was a good ruler.

Illiterate himself, gave precedence to education and established the first school for girls.

Queen Victoria decorated him for his care towards his people.

Constructed Niwas Palace which is the residence of the present Maharana of Mewar, Arvid Singh..

72nd 1874-1884 SAJJAN SINGH   Udaipur

Was Shambhu's cousin and adopted heir.

He came to the throne at the age of 15.

His ascension to throne was contested by his brothers in Bagnor.

Sajjan ordered Man (Gogunda) to provide an army to fight Bagnor.

Built Sajjan Niwas, reformed education and justice systems.

Was keen on history and founded Sajjan Library and History department.

He commissioned the author **Shayamal Das** to write the famous **Vir Vinod**- a history of Mewar.

Requested the local people of Gogunda to set down their history in the "Khyat" from which the second part of this narrative history is based.
He died at the age of 25.

73rd 1884-1930 FATEH SINGH   Udaipur
Was adopted heir of Sajjan, aged 32 when he came to the throne and reigned 46 years.
Treated the British as his servants.
Was decorated for his assistance to England during World War I which was hardly the need to do so as he only supplied 22 camels.
He was heard to instruct the bearer to put the decoration on his horse as it looked better there than on a king.
An austere rigorous person which refused to indulge in the comforts and privileges of court.
His only pastime was hunting which he often did in the hills of Gogunda and Jaswant Garh.
Apart from improving libraries and cultural amenities he created the elegant Shiv Nivas Palace.
Most importantly he introduced the railway and telegraph thus linking Mewar to the rest of India.
In 1921 he was deposed by the British for his lack of cooperation and although he maintained his title, the British placed the administrative power in the hands of his only son Bhupal.

74th 1930-1955 BHUPAL SINGH   Udaipur
Born in 1884 he was given power to rule by the British 10 years before his father's death.
From the age of 16 due to polio and tuberculosis Bhupal spent the rest of his life on a wheelchair.
An advocate for education, himself a keen scholar, and a regard for the safeguarding of the natural environment.
He refused to join Jinnah in his claim to make an independent Muslim state (Pakistan) stating that his ancestors did not falter and neither would he, claiming "I am with India" In 1949 Udaipur joins 22 other cities to form Rajasthan in the Republic of India.

75th 1955-1984 BHAGWAT SINGH   Udaipur
Was adopted by Bhupal at the age of 17, son of Prince Pratap of Bhupalgarh and relative of Fateh of the Sisodia branch.

A country boy, at 19 he was sent to the Palace but life at court was not congenial to him.

By the age of 34 when he succeed Bhuphal, he had adjusted.

However by 1956 the Kingdom of Mewar no longer existed.

In 1971 Indira Ghandi's government rewrote the Constitution and the Maharana found himself becoming an ordinary citizen, an immense taxable estate with a retinue of servants and concubines which he had inherited, to upkeep. He had to earn a living and consequently set up a Private Limited Company and he was in business.

76ᵗʰ 1984 ARVIND SINGH Present Ruler   Udaipur

Was the second born son of Bhagwat. His first, Crown Prince Mahendra, worried that Mewar's inheritance was being sacrificed, filed a civil suit against his father thus cutting himself off from the family.

Now chairman and Trustee of the Mewar Foundation and commercial companies would have been the 76ᵗʰ Maharana of Mewar.

He resides in Shambu Niwas Palace and signs himself simply Arvind Singh, Mewar.

His 'Crown Prince' is LAKSHYA RAJ who will become the 77ᵗʰ Mewar 'Ruler'.

1949 Mewar Joined the Union as the State of Rajasthan with Jaipur as its capital.

B. MAKWANA RAJPUT KIRANTI (Sindh Pakistan) Ancestors of Jhala House Rajput: Raja Palace of Gogunda

Nothing is known of this line of Rajput for the first 1,000 years so the time line of events occurring in SINDH is applicable.

MAKWANA (Rulers) No dates available

1st VEHISADEVA
2nd KERSADEVA c1090 Kersadeva is killed by Sindh's ruler
His son HARPALDEVA flees to Patdi, Gujarat

JHALAWAD in Dhama Gujarat is founded by HARPALDEVA.
He marries a Solanki Rani.
Harpaledeva and/or his son Sodhoji fight with Solanki Ruler against Malwa.

1st HARPALDEVA (Ruler) 1090-1130+
2nd SODHOJI (after 1130)
3rd DURJANSALJI
4th JHAKLDEJI
5th ARJUNSINGHJI
6th DEVRAJJI
7th DUDOJI
8th SURSINGHJI
9th SANTALJI
10th VIJAYPALJI
11th MAGHRAJJI
12th PADAMANSINGH
13th UMENSINGH
14th VEGADJI
15th RAMSINGHJI
16th VIRSINGHJI
17th RANMALGI
The Rathores of Barmar-Kotda attacked and treacherously killed him.

18th SATATSALJI – After 1411
Son of the above renowned chief and made his capital at Mandal.

Revenged his father by ploughing up the site of the above villages with donkeys.

He rebelled three times against the Sultan of Gujarat Ahmed Shah which caused much loss to his kingdom.

19th 1420 JETSINGHJI

Son of the above came to the throne of Jhalawad in 1420.

Continuously attacked by the Sultans of the new Gujarat capital Ahmedabad, he is forced to leave his capital in Patdi and moved to KUWA.

22nd 1469 WHAGHOJI

Was third in line from Jetsingh came to the throne in 1469.

Being rebellious, the son of the Sultan of Gujarat, Prince Khali Khan, attacked him and a severe conflict took place at Sadipur where the Prince was defeated, thereupon the Sultan of Gujarat, MAHMUD, marched upon Kuwa with a large army.

Faced with the alternative of being slain by the Muslims who had turned out in their thousands or starve to death, Wogho Ji decided to persuade the enemy that he was still there, when in effect he was not. But before leaving the Capital, he instructed his numerous Ranis, that while he was out there on the battlefield should he die, and they would know this if his banner fell, they would throw themselves upon a funeral pyre- after of course they had took the pains to see that it was well constructed. Returning to his palace and seeing all his Ranis dead, embarked once more on the battlefield to show the Sultan, he had not finished yet. Waghoji's 8th son Rajodharji succeeded to the throne in1486 as the older brothers fell with their father in battle.

23rd 1486 RAJODHARJI Father of Ajja and Sajja who migrated to Mewar

Laid the foundations in his new capital of HALVAD in 1488.

His first two sons Ajja and SAJJA were by his Idar wife, his third son, Ranoji by his Paramara wife, daughter of Laghdhrji of Muli.

Laghdhrji may have poisoned his son-in-law Rajodhar in order that his daughter's son Ranoji usurps the throne from Ajja and Sajja and become Ruler of Halvad in 1499.

While Ajja and Sajja were on their way to Ahmendabad to seek assistance from the Sultan, Ranoji was proclaimed Ruler of Halvad forcing Ajja and Sajja into exile. First they went to their maternal uncle in Idar (Gujarat) and then to Jodhpur, but not being welcomed they joined the services of Raimal of Mewar.

Ranoji was in turn assassinated by one of his subjects Malik Bakhan,in revenge for having ordered the death of his father and was succeeded by his son Man Singh in 1523.

A successor of Halvad, RAISINGHJI built the fort of DHRANGADHARA in 1730 and the ruler of Halvad, has since then been titled as the Maharaja of Dhrangadhara. The Rajput Jhala line of Gogunda's ancestors now moves to Delwara in Mewar.

DELWARA

Delwara is gifted to SAJJA c 1499-1509 by the Ruler of Mewar, Raimal. AJJA died 1527 at the battle of KHANWA against the first Mughal Emperor BABUR, replacing the wounded SANGA on the field with the Mewar colours.

SAJJA died at the 2nd Sack of Chittor in 1534.

JET SINGH 1534-1567
Son of Sajja. One of his daughters marries Rao Maldeo (1532-1562) of Jodhpur.

But Rao Maldeo seeing her younger sister wanted to marry her instead or as well.

Jet refuses as she is promised to Udai of Mewar, whom she marries and causes enmity between the two rulers.

Another reason being that in 1542 Rao Maldeo forms an alliance with Humayun against Sher Khan where the latter deposes the Mughal Emperor and takes the Empire.

Died at the 3rd Sack of Chittor. His son Man, succeeded him.

MAN SINGH of Delwara 1567-1576
Constructed at Gogunda the Mardana Palace within the labyrinth of a garden and is now the Zenana Mahal (women's quarters)

1560 + CROWN PRINCE PRATAP takes up his Spartan quarters at Gogunda.

1567 Udai and his court take refuge in Gogunda when Akbar takes Chittor.

Man Singh died at the battle of Haldighati 1576 taking the royal insignia in place of Pratap thus saving the Maharana's life.

His elder son Kalyn succeeded him at Delwara. His other son Shatrushal is given Gogunda. The Rajput Jhala line of Gogunda's ancestors now moves to Gogunda in Mewar.

GOGUNDA

1572 GOGUNDA Capital of Mewar

1572 PRATAP I OF MEWAR is crowned at Gogunda which becomes his Capital
Pratap continues to live in hiding in the Aravalli hills between Gogunda and Khumbhalgarh which in turn he uses as Capital of Mewar.
1573 refuses Man Singh of Amber's offer to accept Akbar's sovereignty.
War Council held at Gogunda the night before the Battle of Haldighati
Defeated at Battle of Haldighati: Gogunda is occupied by Akbar's forces.
Pratap retreats to Khumbalgarh.

1st SHATRUSHAL SINGH I 1576 or before
      First Ruler of Gogunda

Lost Gogunda due to dispute with Pratap but also because Gogunda was in the hands of the Mughals.
Patrap Gifted Gogunda To Manmandas Of Badnor c.1580
Shatrushall goes to Jodhpur where the Ruler gives him an estate.
He informs the Ruler of Jodhpur of Mughals advance and a dispute occurs (the Ruler's sister had married Mughal Heir Jahangir)
Shatrushall sets out for Godwar (on Aravalli hills) where his brother Kalyan says Pratap requests his return. Pratap is forced to roam the hills as Mughals poisoned the waters in Kumbhalgarh (1579).
Gogunda continues to be occupied by Mughal forces until 1582.
Under the command of Pratap's son Amar, Mewar's territories are regained at the battle of Diwer (near Haldighati).

SHATRUSHAL returns to render his services to Mewar.

Is wounded fighting against the Mughal Abdula Khan, (1608-9)
Is later killed attacking Imperial Posts at Ravalia.
Gogunda is returned to Shatrushall's son Kanah
Gogunda is captured by the son of Jahangeir (Salim), Khurram 1611

2nd KANAH SINGH I

Crowned 1614 but cannot take possession as Gogunda is occupied by Mughal forces.
Amar sends his maternal uncle Haridas Jhala to negotiate a peace proposal with Prince Khurram
A 'Peace Treaty' is signed at Gogunda between Amar of Mewar and the Mughal Prince Khurram
Kanah Reigned in Gogunda 1619-1668.
Constructed The Temple of Murlidhar (Lord Krishna) and the Temple of Laxi Narayan situated inside the palace.
Rathores set police in Gogunda availing on the claim that Gogunda was gifted to Manmandas (Rathore). Kanah marches on Gogunda, drives away Rathores and removes Ider Police.
Kanah's older brother Nathu, now Gogunda was free, claims throne.
Fathers only son, Jaswant, in old age.
Called by Raj I (Mewar) to fight against Aurangzeb in Aravalli.

3rd JASWANT SINGH I 1668-1689

1684 orders his son Ram to fight against Prince Abkar (Aurangzeb's son) in the Aravallis.
Constructs the Rawala pond (of the palace).
Constructs the temple of Nar Singh Ji.
1685 Orders Ram to expel Rathores who took over Aravallis under Raj I (Mewar) protection

4th RAM SINGH 1689-1710

Is ordered by Jai of Mewar to fight against Aurangzeb's son, Prince Akbar, whose life he spares
Prince Akbar tries to escape through Gogunda but Ram puts sword through the Mughal General.
1683 Ram's daughter marries Amar II Mewar not yet crowned.
Ram attempts to make his 2nd son Vagat Crown Prince because Ajay, his first born had lost an eye.
Sangram II Mewar settles dispute and gives throne to Ajai.

5th AJAI SINGH I 1710-1734
Proved to be a great warrior and faithful to Sangram II of Mewar

6th KANAH SINGH II 1734-1751
Kanah's daughter, Jyot, married Dewlya Kunwar Samat Singh who in 1768 constructed a magnificent temple in Gogunda of Lord Vishnu.
A small temple of Hanuman Ji was built near by.
Two wells were constructed near the Jyot temple and other two in the Mazawad hills.

7th JASWANT SINGH II 1751-I778
Jaswant's daughter marries the 10 years old Raj II of Mewar.
The probable son Ratan, claims the throne of Mewar and leads to civil war.
The revolt failed and Ari of Mewar hunted Jaswant to eliminate him but the Gogunda ruler took refuge in the Aravalli villages.
Constructed Jaswant Garh at Tarawali which being in the Aravalli was unreachable.
Constructed Tarawali Pond, a well and a thana (house).
1770 His son Shatrushal is born in hiding.
In 1772 the British took control of the East Indian Company and the civil war relented.

8th SHATRUSAL SINGH II 1778-1853
Was 7 years old when he came to the throne and ruled for more than 70 years. The investiture ceremony was postponed to later years and was ordered by Bhim possibly under the influence of Col Tod who had taken up residence in the Maharana's palace as the British agent after having driven away the Maratha Peshwa in 1818.
During the Marathas attacks, Shatrushal was forced to take refuge in Jaswant garh, he extended this protection to many farmers, traders and villagers.
Marathas also attacked Jaswant Garh but Shatrushal forced them to retreat.
Shatrushal Sisodian Queen (wife) constructed Har Mandir south of Gogunda, and Chatra Nath Mahadev east of Gogunda.
In 1840 Another queen, Chundawat Begu Ji constructed the temple Chatra Badaneshawar Mahadev inside the palace dedicated to Lord Shiva.

9th LAL SINGH 1853-1863

Born in 1793 was 60 when he came to the throne.

The investiture ceremony did not take place until the year of his death because of lack of finances.

Had settled many disputes during his father's long reign and fought many battles.

When a minister asked Bhim (Mewar) for funds in 1911 the minister was told to rob Gogunda, Lal defeated the attack made upon that occasion.

3 years later some Bhomyas ransacked Gogunda, Lal burned their villages and recovered the animals.

When the villagers refused to pay the tax duty he was always able to settle the matter and establish peace in the area.

Under Sardar's reign, Lal was victim of a conspiracy by one of the Chieftains of Mewar which convinced Shatrushal to remove Lal from court and appoint his younger brother heir.

Later the misunderstanding was cleared.

Took part in a rebellion against Swarup for the increase of tax demanded.

10th MAN SINGH 1863-1891

Marks out the boundaries of Gogunda after a robbery of land took place by the Bhomiyas.

Had to cope with a religious community who were not prepared to pay for village.

1868 Great drought and consequently famine.

Shambhu provided boiled wheat.

Sajjan (Mewar) ordered Man (Gogunda) to provide an army to fight Bagnor.

1871 Man attends a meeting for the reorganizations of boundaries and villages' denomination.

1878-9 A rainfall caused destruction by floods.

The pond of Ranelav in Gogunda had to be repaired.

Two rupees was collected from each household with a contribution from government.

Man Singh was a devotee and often went on pilgrimages.

In 1887 the construction of a temple named Ummed Bihari Ji was started.

Vagheli Ji Posina, Man's wife completed it in 1888.

In 1889 he modernized a temple dedicated to Lord Shiva Nilkanth at Kerva Devra.

Reconstructed the temple of the godess Sitalamata.

Restored the Kunwar Bagh (a garden originated by Man Singh (Shatrushal I father) in the 1570s.

Constructed the following Chhatrias:

DaJi Raj

Raj Rana Lal

Rana Bijapur

Chawan Parsoli

Kunwar Pratap, second son of Jaswant I of Gogunda died in Battle.

11th AJAI SINGH 1891- 1901

At the time of his coronation, Ajay's wife died, he was set in grief and refused to marry again.

In 1885 when still only Crown Prince the marriage of his daughter to the grandson of the ruler of Badnor is recorded at length in the Khyat.

Maharana Fateh often went hunting in Gogunda and at Jaswant Garh.

1891 Constructed the temple Gulab shyam Ji.

He modernized the palace. He constructed stairs in the palace, constructed a new complex north west of the palace, and called it Ajay Niwas.

In 1892 , he gave his adopted son Zuzar a palace of the same name.

In 1894 He restored Jyot Shyam Temple (constructed in 1768 by Kanah I daughter)

Restored the Temple of Murlidhar Ji (Lord Krishna)(constructed in Kanah I time), in memory of Ajay's wife.

1899 a great famine, which was preceded by an earthquake in the middle East and north India, made numerous victims and the value of gold collapsed

12th PRITHVI SINGH 1901- ?

Was Ajay's brother

For the following rulers, no other records are available

13th DALPAT SINGH

14th MANOHAR SINGH

15th BHAIRO SINGH died 27.07.1990

The temple to the god of Mewar, Lord Ekling Ji which is a manifestation of Shiva was inside the palace until the time of the present ruler. His mother,

Bhairo's queen bequeathed the temple to the people and thus this temple was left outside the new boundary walls constructed in 2001 by the Italian architect Remo Serafin.

16th HIMMAT SINGH Last Ruler

ROHIT ASHWA SINGH Crown Prince

January 2001 The Palace was sold to The Human Beings Heritage Co. Pvt Ltd..

Gogunda Palace was recently restored by the Italian Architect Remo Serafin of ARS Studio, Treviso, Italy.

C. SOLANKI RAJPUT GUJARAT

B.C to 130 AD MAURYAN Empire
130-300 KSHATRAPA Empire from Malwa
382-475 GUPTA Empire from Malwa
From 475 to 767 MAITRAK Kingdom of Vallabhi
One of these Rulers: SILADITYA VI is said to be GUHIL'S father.
The queen escaped to Mewar but Kabul forces overtook Gujarat killing the Ruler.

767 – 940 under domain of KABUL

1st 940-995 MULRAJ I
2nd 995-1010 CHAMUDARAJA
3rd 1010 VALLABHARAJA Conquered briefly by Ghaznavid Empire
4th 1010-1022 DURLABHARAJA
5th 1021-1063 BHIMDEV I
6th 1064-1094 KARNADEVA I Accepts services of HARPALDEVA
7th 1094-1125 JAYASINH I Defeats Malwa and takes CHITTORGARH from the Malwa Ruler
8th 1125-1171 KUMARAPALA
9th 1171-1176 AJAYAPALA
10th 1176-1178 MULRAJAVA

1196 Ghuri conquers Northern India including Gujarat

1207 Chittor ruled by Chalyukas (Solanki)

11th JAYASINH II
12th BHIMA II died 1242
13th TRIBUVANPAL died 1244

1243 SOLANKIS lost control of Gujarat to their Feudatories, the VAGHLEA chiefs of DHOLKA

1st VISALA 1244
2nd ARJUNA 1262
3rd SARANGADEVA 1275
4th KARNADEVA II 1297-1304

1292 The Vaghleas become tributaries of the Yadava dynasty of Devagiri in the Deccan.
Gujarat is taken over by the Delhi Sultanate.

DELHI SULTANATE 1304-1391

1297-8 ALA-UD-DIN CONQUERS GUJARAT
Gujarat is incorporated in the Delhi Sultanate.
Ruled by Muslim Governor till 1411.
Gujarat's Muslim Governor ZAFAR KHAN MUZAFFAR asserts his independence from the Delhi Sultanate.

ZAFARID RULERS:

Zafar Khan 1391-1403
Muhammad Shah I Tatar 1403-1407
Muzaffar Shah 1407-1411
AHMED Shah 1411-1442
Established AHMEDABAD as the capital

1437 The Sultan combines forces with the Sultan of Malwa to attack Mewar but are defeated.

1458 QUTUB-DIN (DAWUD KHAN)
attacks Chittor and is defeated.

MAHMUD SHAH I BEGRA SAIF AD-DIN 1458-1511
1499 AJJA and SAJJA seeks the aid of the Sultan of Gujarat but are exiled from Halvad before they can do so .

MUZAFFAR SHAH II 1511-1526
SIKANDAR 1526-1526
MAHMUD SHAH II 1526-1526
BAHADUR SHAH 1526-1535
Delhi Sultanate is overcome by the Mughal Empire

To the Mughal Empire 1535-1536

BAHADUR SHAH **Delhi Sultanate restored** 1536-1537
MAHMUD SHAH III 1537-1554
AHMAD SHAH III 1554-1561
MUZAFFAR SHAH III 1561-1573

1574 AKBAR conquerors GUJARAT

1583 MUZZAFAR SHAH III restored

1583-1728 The MUGHAL EMPIRE

1720-1818
The MARATHA CONFEDERACY

1818-1948 The
BRITISH EMPIRE

1948 The BHARAT UNION OF INDIA

D. PARAMARA RAJPUT MALWA (Pradesh)

320-187 BC MAURYAN Empire
119-380 AD KSHATRPA Empire
395-750 GUPTA Empire

During this period they conquer Gujarat and much of Mewar making CHITTORGARH their capital, built by CHITRANG Maun MORI a RAJPUT Chieftain.

Bappa Rawal as Prince Kalbhoj, claims Mewar as his kingdom including Chitttor conquered by Malwa.
He charms the people and his uncle Mori who makes him his general when Malwa is attacked by the Arab Caliphate.
The nobles dethrone Mori and Kalbhoj takes over Chittor.

948-974 SIYAKA II takes CHITTORGARH
974-995 VAKPATIRAJA
995-1010 SINDHURAJA
1010-1055 BHOJA I
1055-1060 JAYASIMHA
1060-1087 UDAYADITYA
1087- 1097 LAKSHMANADEVA
Defeated by SOLANKI, JHALAWAD rulers and loses CHITTOR

1097- 1134 NARAVARMAN
1134- 1142 YASOVARMAN
1142-1160 JAYAVARMAN I
1160-1193 VINDHYAVARMAN
1193-1210 SUBHATAVARMAN
1210-1218 ARJUNAVAEMAN I
1218-1239 DEVAPALA

1243 c Regain Chittor from Solanki (Gujarat) only to lose it to Jaitra of Mewar

1239-1256 JAITUGIDEVA
1256-1269 JAYAVARMAN II
1269-1274 JAYASIMBHA

1274- 1283 ARJUNAVARMAN II
1283-…. BHOJA II

MAHLAKADEVA died c 1305

1305 ALA-UD-DIN conquers MALWA which remained in the hands of
the DELHI Sultanate till 1390
1332 start of the Black Death (Bubonic plague)

GHURID replaces PARAMARA clan

1390-1405 DILAWAR KHAN HUSAIN Sultan
1405-1435 ALP KHAN HUSHANG
CHONDA removed as Regent (Mewar) retires to MANDU capital of
Malwa.
1435-6 GHAZNI KHAN MUHAMMD
1436 MAS-UD KHAN

KHALJI

1436-1469 MAHMUD SHAH I
1437 The Sultan made six unsuccessful raids on MEWAR
1469-1500 GHIYAS-UD-DIN SHAH Sultan
1500-1511 NASR SHAH
1511-1531 MAMUD SHAH II

1531-1535 conquered by BAHADUR SHAH of GUJARAT

1535-1542 QADIR SHAH

1542-1555 conquered by the MUGHAL Empire

1555 SHAJA-AT KHAN
1555-1562 MIYAN BAYEZID BAZ BAHADUR
Took refuge at Chittor as Udai II guest when Akbar attacked

1562-1720 THE MUGHAL EMPIRE

1720-1818

The MARATHA CONFEDERACY

1818-1948 The
BRITISH EMPIRE

1948 The BHARAT UNION OF INDIA

E. SIMULTANEOUS FOREIGN RULE IN INDIA

SINDH (Pakistan)

520-326 BC The Indus Valley Civilization- Persian Domain
306-250 BC MAURYAN Empire
230 AD Kushanshas
410 White Huns
600's Chach

712-830's AMIRS of Sindh under the CALIPHATE
The HIBARI Clan ruled from 850-1005

1005-1058 Conquered by the GHAZNAVID Empire (Afghanistan) Mughal

1025-1053 SUMRA
1053-1058 BHUNGAR
1068-1092 DUDA I (Kills 2nd Makwana Ruler
1092-1107 SINGHAR
SUMRA Clan continues with: HAMUN (female),
PITHU KHAIRA, HAFIF I, UMAR,
DUDA II, PAHTU, GENHRA II,
MOHAMMED TURGENHRA II

Other Sindh rulers continued until

THE MUGHAL EMPIRE,
followed by:
AFGHASISTAN RULE,
BRITISH RULE

DELHI RULERS
(Muslim)

1162 MOHAMMAD GHURI (a Turk from Afghanistan) uses Punjab as base to conquer northern India which leads to:

1191-2 Chauhan ruler (of Delhi) PRITHVIRAJ III and RAJPUT confederation including Mewar defeated by MOHAMMED GHURI

1st SLAVE Dymasty

1193-1206 MOHAMMED OF GHUR 1206 GHURI Assassinated
1206-1210 QUTUB-UD-DIN AIBAK
1210-1210 ARAM Shah
1210-1236 SHAMS-UD-DIN-ILTUTMISH. Destroys NAGDA
1236-1236 RUKN-UD-DIN FIROZ SHAH I
1236-1240 RAZIYYAT, ILTUTMISH'S DAUGHTER
1240-1242 MUIZ-UD-DIN BAHRAM SHAH
1242-1246 ALA-UD-DIN MASUT
1246-1266 NASIR-UD-DIN MAHMUD SHAH I
1266-1287 MUIZ-UD-DIN KUBAD

2nd KHILJI Dynasty

1290-1296 JALAL-UD-DIN FIROZ SHAH II
1296-1296 RUKN-UD-DIN IBRAHIM SHAH I
1296-1316 ALA-UD-DIN KHILJI

Aug 15 1303 the Sultan takes CHITTOR and slaughters RATAN and thousands of warriors. The women commit a gigantic jauhar.
The Sultan appoints his son KHIJR KHAN governor of Mewar.
1314 ALLAUDIN replaces son with Rajput MALDEO at Chittor
1316 Ala-ud-Din dies and is replaced by:

1316-1316 SIHAB-UD-DIN UMAR SHAH
1316-1320 QUTUB-UD-DIN MUBARAK SHAH I
1320 NASIR-UD-DIN KHSRU SHAH
The Khilji Dynasty collapsed and is replaced by:

3rd TUGHLUQ Dynasty

1320-1325 GHIYAS-UD-DIN TUGHLUG SHAH I
1325-1351 MUHAMMAD II IBN TUGHLUQ
1351-1388 FIROZ SHAH III
1388-1388 TUGHLUQ SHAH II

1389-1394 MUHAMMAD SHAH III
1394-1394 SIKANDER SHAH I
1394-1395 MAHMUD SHAH II
1395-1398 NASRAT SHAH
Timur destroys Delhi
1398-1412 MAHMUD SHAH (restored)
1412-1414 DAULAT KHAN LODI

4th SAYYID Dynasty

1414-1421 KHIZR KHAN
1421-1434 MUIZ-UD-DIN MUBARAK
1434-1443 MUHAMMAD SHAH IV
1443-1451 ALAM SHAH

5th LODI Dynasty

1451- 1488 BUHLUL
1488-1517 SIKANDER II
Destroys Mathura shrines.
Makes AGRA his capital.

1517-1526 IBRAHIM II
Is defeated by BABUR at the battle of Panipat1526 bringing an end to the Lodi Sultanate and establishing the Mughal Empire in India.
MUGHAL EMPERORS
DELHI/AGRA

1526-1530 BABUR Founder
1527 Overcomes Mewar at the battle of Khanwaha
1530-1540 HUMAYUN

SUR Dynasty

1540 SHER SHAH (Sher Khan)
Is ancestor of Hakim Khan mentioned in Battle of Haldighati Roll of Honour
1542 conquers North India.
Humayun escapes to Persia

1545-1552 ISALAM SHAH
1552-1553 ADIL SHAH
1553-1554 IBRAHIM SUR
1554-1555 SIKANDER SHAH II

MUGHAL DYNASTY Reinstated

1555-1556 HUMAYUN restored

1556-1605 AKBAR
becomes emperor age 13

AKBAR ATTACKS MEWAR and causes the 3rd Sack of Chittor in 1567-8
Constructed well near Gogunda.
Man Singh of Amber (Jaipur) b.1540 d.1579 fights with Akbar's son Salim against Pratap.
The sister of Man Singh's father, Raja Bhagwan Das 1574-1589, had married Akbar in c.1562.
1587 Akbar ceases to attack Mewar: focuses on the Northwest and PUNJAB

1605-1627 JAHANGIR (SALIM)
Renews attacks on Mewar
1586 Married a daughter of Ruler of Jodhpur, she died in 1604
His son Khurram Captured Gogunda 1611.
Mughals occupied Gogunda.

1627-1658 SHAH JAHAN (Khurram)
Was not eldest son but the brothers ahead of him were 'removed'
Before becoming emperor in 1627 he sought exile at the court of Karen of Mewar who made Jag Mandir available to the then Prince Khurram.
Built the Taj Mahal to commemorate his wife Mumtaz Mahal who died giving birth to their 14th son.

1658-1707 AURANGZEB
Imprisons his father Shah Jahan and takes throne sets massive attack on Mewar

1707-1712 BAHADUR SHAH
1712-1718 JAHANDAR SHAH

1718-1719 FARRUKHSIYAR
1719-1754 MUHAMMAD SHAH
1754-1759 ALAMGIR II
1759-1736 SHAH ALAM
Nominal Emperor until his death1806- ended Mughal dynasty.

1736 MARATHA BAJI RAO captures UDAIPUR

BRITISH INDIA- DELHI

1751 Robert Clive captures Arcot.
1756 British rule in Bengal.
1764 British and Indian Troops defeat Mughal Rulers.
1765 Clive returns as Governor of Bengal.
1772 British East Co. replaced by British Govt. of India.

Marathas advance

1773 Regulation Act- Warren Hastings becomes Governor General.
1775 First Anglo-Indian war to break Maratha's coalition.
1788 Marathas defeat Udaipur.
1794 Mewar attacks Marathas.

Capt. Tod's first visit to Mewar

1813 Mewar looted by Amir Khan.
1818 Final British victory over Marathas.
Mewar signs Treaty with British.
Tod becomes 1st British Agent in Mewar.
1823 Administration of Mewar taken over by British.
1876 Sajjan Singh given full rights to govern Mewar.
1877 Queen Victoria Empress of India.
1921 British curtail Maharana's power.
1947 Indian Independence

Mewar Joins the Indian Union.

1949 Udaipur and former Princely States joins Union as Rajastan

Glossary

Bagh - garden

Bahadur - hero

Bapa - father

Brahmin - Indian Priest

Chawans - they were men on horseback who offered their services to the Ruler

Chhatra/i - can be a pavilion with dome or a monument used as a memorial

Chowk - courtyard

Darbar - Ruler or royal assembly

Dayiya - a noble Rajput

Garh - fort

Haveli - mansion

Jagir - an assignment of land

Kafiyat - a historical poem in Mewari dialect also *Khyat*

Kumari - title of Princess

Kunwar - title of Prince when used as a prefix- princess when used as a suffix

Laximi - goddess, wife of a god

Magri - hill

Maha - Great

Mahal - a palace

Maharaja - Rajput King

Maharana - King of Kings, title of Merwar Ruler

Mandir - palace or temple

Marathas - Hindu warriors who first sought the liberation from foreign Rule but then plundered it's own kind to obtain dominion

Mardana - men's quarters

Nawab - title of Muslim ruler or prince

Nazrana - ceremony of gifts

Niwas - Palace

Paramara - Rajput clan of Malwa (now Pradesh area)

paravana - letter or document

patta - document

pol - gate

Rahat - place for a well

Raj - pertaining to a Rajput or head of state

Raja - ruling king, title of Ruler of Gogunda

Rajmata - Queen Mother
Rajput - warrior caste, Son of King
Rana - short term for Rulers of Merwar
Rani - Queen
Rao - title of Rathore King or Baron
Rathore - Rajput clan of Marwar- Jodhpur and Gujarat
Rawla /Rawula - Residence of a noble
Sardar - Rajput Chieftan
Sati - self-immolation of a widow on her husband's funeral pyre
Shah - Title of a Mughal (Persian or Islamic) King
Shaktawats - were the descendants of Udai II rebellious second son, **Sakta** who defected to the Mughals and the clan are the continuous rivals of the **Choondawats**, descendants of Lakha's Crown Prince **Choonda** who was deprived of his right to rule in favour of his younger step-brother Mokal.
Shri - term to address a honourable being
Talwar Bandhai - sword ceremony of a newly crowned king
Thakur - Lord
Thana - a sort of military police station
Thikanas - chief town of a group of villages
Umaro - head of a state in Mewar
Zenana - women's quarters

Lightning Source UK Ltd.
Milton Keynes UK
13 April 2010
152709UK00003B/1/P